# Before They Say
# Goodbye

David Sawler

Unless otherwise indicated, all Scripture quotations are taken from the Holy Bible, New Living Translation, copyright © 1996, 2004, 2007 by Tyndale House Foundation. Used by permission of Tyndale House Publishers, Inc., Carol Stream, Illinois 60188. All rights reserved. Scripture quotations marked (NIV) are taken from the Holy Bible, New International Version®, NIV®. Copyright © 1973, 1978, 1984, 2011 by Biblica, Inc.™ Used by permission of Zondervan. All rights reserved worldwide.

Graphic designer: Jason Eyre

Cover photo: Jordan Mattie (www.choicephotoanddesign.com)

Model: Rob Reid

ISBN: 978-1-77069-293-0

Printed in Canada

Word Alive Press
131 Cordite Road, Winnipeg, MB R3W 1S1
www.wordalivepress.ca

Library and Archives Canada Cataloguing in Publication

Sawler, David
    Before they say goodbye / David Sawler.

ISBN 978-1-77069-293-0

    1. Church work with youth. 2. Youth--Religious life.3. Church attendance. I. Title.

BV4447.S238 2011          259'.2          C2011-903258-9

[To my family, who are my purpose.]

# Table of Contents

Intro

# Intro

And what do you benefit if you gain the whole world
but lose your own soul? Is anything worth more than
your soul?

– Matthew 16:26

## Losing

I hate losing things. I seem to be constantly losing my car keys. If I look around enough, check my pockets, peer under the couch cushions, or just retrace my steps, sooner or later I find them. Or even more likely, my wife finds them for me. However, sometimes we lose things that are far more valuable than a set of keys. Some of the things we lose are never to be found.

It seems that many churches are losing people at an unacceptable rate. This seems especially true when it comes to our youth and young adults. It is apparent that the majority of the children and youth who have either grown up in the church, or have attended for a time, are more likely to not become active adults in our churches than to remain.

There is nothing easy about raising children and young people. After working with youth and young adults for fifteen years, I have certainly discovered a few things. The first is, I am not always sure what to do. I think anyone who claims they do is very likely lying or semi-delusional. As we have now raised some of our children into adulthood I cannot even believe I ever gave parents advice on how to raise their own children. I have discovered that all the years of working with young people didn't adequately prepare me to raise my own. I have still been challenged, broken, frustrated, and left feeling lost without any clear direction at times.

As I have travelled and spoken to thousands of youth, young adults, leaders, ministers, and parents, I have sensed that many have felt the same way. Over the past years, we have dedicated ourselves to telling the stories of young people who have either grown up in the church, or attended for a time, but have left. Many people have identified with the stories and have been challenged to reconnect with their churches and faith.

As a father, there is nothing I want more than to see my children walking in everything God has for them. I would like to see each of them become a person who is a blessing to those around them, no matter where they end up in life. I want my children to succeed. I do not want to see them lost.

Whether you are a parent, a church leader of some kind, or minister, God has called you to be a part of the spiritual upbringing of this generation. It is not enough to have great buildings, programs, and the right music. We seem to have gained so much, yet we are losing the souls of this generation. My prayer for you as you start this book is that God would speak to you about your role in in both reaching and keeping those around you.

## Depressing Wisdom?

In the Old Testament book of Ecclesiastes, Solomon writes that through his experience he came to the conclusion that most things in life are meaningless. It seems Solomon even has a scale of meaninglessness. He tells one story of something that is not just meaningless, but also depressing.

> This is the case of a man who is all alone, without a child or a brother, yet who works hard to gain as much wealth as he can. But then he asks himself, "Who am I working for? Why am I giving up so much pleasure now?" It is all so meaningless and depressing. (Ecclesiastes 4:8)

Many families, ministries, and churches are finding themselves in this place. On any given Sunday, a church can gather together and look around and see almost all grey hair. Too often, whether it is ever vocalized or not, a depression sets over that group as they know their days are numbered, and there is no one to pass what they have on to. They may have gained the whole world, but now feel they have lost what is most important—a future.

When faced with the facts of the Western church's retention rates, we can become overwhelmed, worried, frightened, and start questioning God on how this can even be happening. However, not everything is as it seems at first glance. In fact, while what you are about to read may be challenging, it is not meant to be depressing. The church is not dying. Are there things we need to understand and change? Of course there are. However, I believe God may even be behind much of what is happening, which I will explain as we go through this book.

## Why Read This Book?

This book, like any one book, will not answer or speak to all the issues that are facing this generation. It is, however, intended to make you think about your own family and ministry, to make you examine the long-term effect of what you are spending your time and energy doing, and to help you know and understand some of the things that will try to rob the faith of this generation.

I believe you will also be encouraged with stories of hope and see how God is, in fact, working in the midst of our struggles. The material presented here is not written to merely state obvious problems, but to help put some tools into your hands that you can use with those you are leading. This is meant to be a book of hope, direction, and encouragement for everyone who is dealing with the new generation.

One of the verses we have based this book on, as well as previous ones, is John 15:16, which states, *"You did not choose me, but I chose you and appointed you to go and bear fruit—fruit that will*

*last. Then the Father will give you whatever you ask in my name"*
(NIV). God has not simply called us to live lives that bear fruit,
but rather we are to bear fruit that lasts. If there is something I am
asking for today, it is that this generation hears, sees, experiences,
and comes to a saving knowledge of Jesus Christ.

## The Format

The premise of this book is simple. First, it is to help you understand some of the things that are robbing this generation of its
faith and joy as believers. In Luke 8, we can read the story of the
sower.

> One day Jesus told a story in the form of a parable
> to a large crowd that had gathered from many towns
> to hear him: "A farmer went out to plant his seed.
> As he scattered it across his field, some seed fell on a
> footpath, where it was stepped on, and the birds ate
> it. Other seed fell among rocks. It began to grow, but
> the plant soon wilted and died for lack of moisture.
> Other seed fell among thorns that grew up with it and
> choked out the tender plants. Still other seed fell on
> fertile soil. This seed grew and produced a crop that
> was a hundred times as much as had been planted!"
> When he had said this, he called out, "Anyone with
> ears to hear should listen and understand…
>
> "This is the meaning of the parable: The seed is God's
> word. The seeds that fell on the footpath represent
> those who hear the message, only to have the devil

come and take it away from their hearts and prevent them from believing and being saved. The seeds on the rocky soil represent those who hear the message and receive it with joy. But since they don't have deep roots, they believe for a while, then they fall away when they face temptation. The seeds that fell among the thorns represent those who hear the message, but all too quickly the message is crowded out by the cares and riches and pleasures of this life. And so they never grow into maturity. And the seeds that fell on the good soil represent honest, good-hearted people who hear God's word, cling to it, and patiently produce a huge harvest." (Luke 8:4–8, 11–15)

It is through scriptures like these that we can learn that there will be many things in this life that will rob, kill, and destroy the seed that is planted. Through the following chapters, we will discuss what these paths, rocks, and thorns represent in today's world. Many of the issues which our children and youth are saying are robbing them of their faith are discussed in the following pages.

However, this book is not just meant to talk about obvious problems and issues. We will also hear from many pastors, teachers, church leaders, and ministry leaders from around the world. They will give us advice on how we can to deal with each of these issues. Also, we will hear stories of ministries who are having some measure of success in dealing with many of these issues. We believe this will inspire hope, provide practical ideas, and help you consider what you could do in each of your own situations.

> All the text in these boxes are quotes from youth and young adults who grew up attending church.

What is unique about this book is that we are addressing what you can do to prevent people from walking away. *Before They Say Goodbye* is an attempt to be proactive. This book is intended to be a practical source of ideas and advice for parents, leaders, and ministers. It is intended to point you to real ways we can help keep our children and youth now attending church strong in their faith. We are not promoting a program or promising that if you do exactly what one of the leaders has done in the book, it will work everywhere. We do believe, however, that this can be a tool that helps you, equips you, and encourages you to bear fruit that remains.

# Why Church?

01

# Why Church?

# 01

## Loving the Church

I love the church. I even love the church I am a part of now. I am all too aware this is not the view or experience of everyone. In fact, when most people even hear the word "church," it brings up thoughts and emotions that aren't very favourable.

There is something that churches need to hear, even if they don't want to. The vast majority of people who have left your churches do not want to come back. Many are very happy they left. For some who have been hurt by the church, the anger, resentment, confusion, and disappointment stops them from coming back. Those who are now agnostic, atheists, indifferent, or not sure what they are seem very content without a return to their old churches. Even the belief that most will just leave for a time and then come back when they are married, have children, or settle down is completely false. They are not all coming back, not even a majority of them. In fact, most don't.

> **"**
> For now I want to *be* the church, not attend one. I feel this is a work of my God to bring me out of it. I thank Him every day.
> **"**

There is also no truth to the thought that all who leave traditional churches are walking away from God. In fact, I believe many have left in pursuit of God and a real faith community. The number of people meeting today in various forms of faith communities is growing while many traditional church models are shrinking. Because so many traditional churches are struggling with retaining their young people, however, we have been led to believe that most of those in the younger generation have left the faith. This is not totally accurate. There are certainly too many who have walked away from their faith, but there is also a great number who in have no way walked away from God. In the coming decades, the number of people in home or organic, faith communities will continue to grow. Someday, they may outnumber those in traditional churches, demonstrating how large this reformation is.

I have one friend who I attended Bible college with many years ago. At the time, she shared the following message with me:

> A friend shared with us about simple/organic/home church and it turned my life upside-down. I officially left the "institutional" church and haven't looked back. A *lot* of mind-blowing Kingdom stuff has happened in our lives since then. I can honestly say that I don't think I will ever be a part of a traditional church again, since experiencing the life-giving power of living in community with other believers and building Christ's Kingdom outside the walls of traditional church. My life has never been the same since… in a fantastic way.

This is the story of millions of people today.

> **"**
> **I can't find a church that notices or cares if I don't come back… and that is even after attending for several months or years.**
> **"**

When I say I love the church, what I mean is that I love what the church is. It is a body of people dedicated to loving God and their neighbours. It is people united together to pursue everything that is pure, holy, and good. It is a place to find mercy, grace, acceptance, forgiveness, wholeness, healing, and love. It is where we are equipped with everything we need to pursue and experience life to the fullest. It is where we worship, where we have community, a place of friends, and a place of purpose. It is where we experience Jesus. It is how we live out His mission.

While this is my definition, it is certainly not everyone's experience. Even in writing this book and speaking about these topics, my goal isn't necessarily to get youth and young adults back in the doors of ministries they have left. It is very possible that they will never be interested in coming back. Perhaps it would be best for some of them if they didn't. It would seem some must leave and have a time of healing in order that they can find Him again.

> **"**
> **We both grew up in the church—with parents who were ministers—and we both used to genuinely believe in the church. We don't believe in the church anymore, but we believe in God, Jesus, love, and a community of followers more than ever!**
> **"**

When we think of our own definition of church, it is clouded by our own experiences. There are too many reasons people hate or are disillusioned with the church today. People have experienced things that are far from Christlikeness—people and leaders fighting for power, gossip, judgement, backstabbing, boredom, and the like.

However, it is impossible to be a Christian and not be part of the church. Many have tried to live their Christian walk alone, but we are called to live out our lives together. Very few who have decided to walk their faith journey alone finish their walk strong, if at all. At best, it is a shadow of what was meant to be.

One of the biggest issues we face today is that this generation sees almost no connection to living like Jesus and attending services. In fact, many can't even find a connection at all. Here is an email I received which sums up the feelings of many in this generation:

> Go ahead and go. If you want to go, then you'll be miserable staying and of no help to anyone, and there's no room on this bus for people who refuse to pull their weight. Think I'm being harsh? Sometimes the best thing a person who is sick and tired of church and/or church life can do i see what it's like on "the other side."
>
> When you go, listen to the people you meet—really listen. Don't just look at their outsides, their lifestyles, or their choices; get to know them and ask them questions. Think about what you yourself are experiencing. Ask yourself if what you find was what you expected. Get church out of your system. But then, once you do, if you miss Him, look for Jesus, because where you're going is where He already is.
>
> He doesn't inhabit the comfortable, cushy pews, or the gossipy conversations in the lobby, or the fake smiles. He's in the wild places, the places where there are desperate people doing desperate things at a desperate pace, trying desperately to find peace. Take a

good look at those people, because you will have the choice to be one of them, in short order.

And if you decide that you *do* want to be with Him, then remember this: there are all kinds of people who follow Him in all kinds of different ways—their only connection is the goal of loving Him and others. If you ask Him, He will help you find a community of people who will be the best friends you have ever had, and go on the craziest sorts of adventures. But you probably don't believe me yet, so maybe you should go ahead and go, and try to forget what I've told you.

– Brian Ballinger

This generation is looking for something real. If they do not find it in the church they grew up in, most will not stay. While I do not think it is a totally correct attitude, these people have almost zero commitment to past structures, which seem irrelevant or stuck in the past. The present generation also has almost little or no denominational ties or prejudices.

## Our Definition of Church Must Change

I use statistics a lot when I speak. However, I disagree with many of the statistics on church retention. There are a vast majority who simply focus on service attendance numbers. If church attendance alone is the marker we are to use for Christian maturity, it is a poor goal. I say that because the longer a person attends the majority of traditional churches, the less likely they are to share

> **"** I left 'church' over eight years ago, and it probably saved my relationship with Jesus. **"**

their faith, have any non-Christian friends, or even bring someone to their church. It is impossible to become more like Jesus and become less fruitful.

If we could simply be what the Bible says a church should be, people would be attracted to it. Far fewer would ever want to leave it. We need the church; we need to be a part of it. However, we do not necessarily need all or most of the forms, functions, traditions, rituals, programs, denominations, or philosophies of many churches. Most of these are just ways people have tried to live out what we are called to be. But they are just things; they are not the church.

The church is living, breathing, flowing, moving, and evolving. The church is you. The church is us. We are the Temple of the Holy Spirit. It is love, because God is love. It is full of grace, mercy, and truth because He resides there, and that is what He is. Church was never meant to be, and cannot be, confined to a building, location, or to just one denomination. The church is powerful. Even the gates of hell cannot overcome it.

It is evident that many people's faith is wrapped up in just attending services. However, the church is not simply a place to attend services. Joining in corporate worship or teaching times may be one of the outflows of our Christian walk, but it does not have

to be the pinnacle event. In fact, for most of the younger generations, it is not. It may be hard to admit, but everyone will not connect with your church or the way you connect to God. In humanity and through scripture, we learn that different people connect
in different ways, because God made us unique. Some people will
thrive in the quiet, some will enjoy deep theology, some will enjoy
connecting to God in nature, or in worship, or through shock-
and-awe services. There is almost infinite diversity.

## Meeting Together?

In the book of Hebrews, we are told about the importance of
being together. *"And let us not neglect our meeting together, as some
people do, but encourage one another, especially now that the day
of his return is drawing near"* (Hebrews 10:25) This is one of the
key verses used to back up the importance of attending services.
However, that teaching may be taking this verse out of its proper
context. First, if you study the book of Acts and most of the letters to the early church, you will discover how the early Christians
understood this in their own context.

First, they did meet in the temple. There was time for teaching,
worship, and reverence. They also met daily, though. The primary
location for this was not in the temple, but in people's homes. It
was in the homes of believers that the church ate together, shared
together, grew together, and discussed things together. And
through this, the people became family. It may be more true to
scripture to say that we are to be meeting together daily in each

other's homes rather than just attending services together. After all, the majority of the early church's gatherings took place in homes.

These two views likely represent the main philosophy differences between the traditional church and the home church movement. But either of these interpretations can still miss the point. In fact, there are very healthy traditional churches, ones that are growing, ministering, and reaching the communities they are in. The same can be said of many home/organic churches. At the same time, both have lots of areas in which they could be more effective.

It is not all about location. Rather, are we being what the church was intended to be wherever we are? The outflows and practices may look different, but there are some things a church must be doing to be healthy, attractive, and a place for people to grow and stay. If our goal is to just get people back to a location, we are going to fail. Our focus needs to be on helping people connect to God and find a community of faith—whether or not it is ours.

### Beautiful Church?

What are we to do? What are we to be for others? What are we to *be* as a group of people? For a moment, let's wipe the slate clean and pretend we don't know anything about our own church background. Let's look at a few scriptures that give instruction of what we are to be and do. I believe there is hardly a person out there who wouldn't want to be in a community like the one I am about to describe.

First, the church is not a group of people who attend services together. The church is foremost to be a covenant community— or, in other words, a community that is committed to the growth, provision, and care of all its members. It's incredible that this generation has discovered the shallowness of many church settings while others seem blind to it. It is only when we realize that we are called to do more than just meet with each other that we can begin to understand why some people leave in search of something more meaningful. If we begin to think of ourselves as a covenant community, we can see how so many scriptures begin to take on their full meaning.

> **❝**
> I'm more satisfied with life now than when I was attending a church. I haven't missed it. I find people are nicer, more welcoming elsewhere. I get more value, live a full life, and experience more than sitting in a pew. I've chosen to find God in the everyday things—not just on Sundays.
> **❞**

Scripture tells us that there are things we must do for each other. The first one, which is the foundation for the rest, is love. Jesus even said, *"Your love for one another will prove to the world that you are my disciples"* (John 13:35). Sadly, this is not what many faith communities are known for. It has to be the goal of the church. If we are known for something else before this one, we are wrong and in error. Love is not even presented as an option for anyone who says they are a Christ follower. We are actually commanded to love. *"Love means doing what God has commanded us, and he has commanded us to love one another, just as you heard from the beginning"* (2 John 1:6)

Love is completely necessary if we are going to enter into a covenant community. The truth is, it is not easy to love everyone. Love is a fruit of the Spirit. We need to ask God to increase it in our lives. We need it if we are going to work out of pure and Godly motives. In 1 John 3:16 we read, *"We know what real love is because Jesus gave up his life for us. So we also ought to give up our lives for our brothers and sisters."* If we just get this one part right, the church will become a place where covenant community works.

In the scriptures, we are told a story which demonstrates what a covenant looks like. It is the story of two young men, David and Jonathan. David was to be king, while Jonathan was the son of the present king, Saul. After the success David had fighting giants and many other foes, Saul became jealous to the point of trying to kill David. However, David and Jonathan became friends. In 1 Samuel we read:

> After David had finished talking with Saul, he met Jonathan, the king's son. There was an immediate bond between them, for Jonathan loved David... And Jonathan made a solemn pact with David, because he loved him as he loved himself. (1 Samuel 18:1, 3)

True covenants, and covenant communities, work because they are birthed in love. Jonathan vowed to try and keep David from harm, and he did just that on many occasions. The covenant they made meant Jonathan actually lived out what it means to lay down one's live for another. Consider, though, that Jonathan knew the talk that his own father had heard about David. Yes, Saul had killed his thousands, but David his tens of thousands. By remaining in this covenant and protecting David, Jonathan would have to have known that it would cause himself to never be king.

Church is meant to be free of selfish ambition and people seeking power. We are a community of people who are to serve, love, and be dedicated to the success of those around us. In Acts, we read:

> They worshiped together at the Temple each day, met in homes for the Lord's Supper, and shared their meals with great joy and generosity—all the while praising God and enjoying the goodwill of all the people. And each day the Lord added to their fellowship those who were being saved. (Acts 2:46–47)

It is impossible to be with people continually, to share with and be generous without there being connections. Just as Jesus spent time with His disciples, the early believers continued this practice. They spent their time listening, ministering, teaching, eating, laughing, crying, and just living life.

A covenant community is one that is expressed through relationship with other people. It is possible to attend church services and never be in this type of community. This is one reason people that leave. Scripture teaches that we are to be in covenant. People long for it. The church is a place for people to connect with other people. Just as the disciples could ask questions, you need to be able to do the same. Church is a place where you should be able to pour into people, and people will pour into you. It is a place so safe that you can *"confess your sins to each other and pray for each other so that you may be healed"* (James 5:16).

If any generation has missed out on the opportunity to be in this type of faith community, they have missed out on seeing the full picture of what the church is. They are actually being robbed of the healing and growth that occurs when confession and forgiveness take place. Instead of the judgement so many have found inside church walls, imagine they discovered people who would *"make allowance for each other's faults, and forgive anyone who offends you. Remember, the Lord forgave you, so you must forgive others"* (Colossians 3:13). In covenant communities, there is a true understanding of what it means to be the family of God. These communities, just like families, accept the imperfections and uniqueness of its own members, while helping them to grow.

In covenant, we even surround the weak and the new. All members are valued, important, and needed. 1 Thessalonians 5:11 says, *"So encourage each other and build each other up, just as you are already doing."* The church is a place of growth. This happens through the work of the Spirit, the teaching we receive, and the prayer and encouragement of others. Hebrews 10:24 says, *"Let us think of ways to motivate one another to acts of love and good works."* The church is a place to be lifted up, encouraged, built up, pushed, and sent.

The church, as a covenant community, is beautiful. It is what so many are longing for. They have heard about it. They have read about it. They have dreamed about it. For many, though, it has been elusive, and they are unsure if it even exists. However, countless youth, young adults, and adults have left in search of it.

Our goal needs to be to help connect this generation to a place where the church is living as a covenant community. They need to have, just as we do, a place where we can confess our sins to one another—a place where they are encouraged, built up, and prayed for. As parents and leaders, we need to make sure this is what we are. We need to be this church. We need to live out these scriptures. If we are in error—whether in gossip, disunity, or seeking power—we need to repent openly. This new generation is worth far more than our pride. Be the church.

### Advice

Pray that God would truly make you a person who people can share with, confess their sins to, receive encouragement from, and get prayer from. Ask God to fill you with His love.

**FOR PARENTS.** We first have to model love for God and the church (people) in our homes. Do we invite people into our homes or activities? Are our conversations with believers about building each other up or things that are good, pure, and holy? Our children's perception of the church is formed by our words and actions.

**FOR PASTORS.** As pastors, one of our callings is to protect those under our care. In all we do, we need to make sure our churches are known for love first. Preach it, live it, and protect people from harm.

# Generational Ministry

02

# Generational Ministry

# 02

I spent thirteen years of my life as a youth and young adult pastor. Being a minister for these age groups may be challenging, but is also extremely rewarding. Working with youth requires a large measure of grace, time, patience, sacrifice, endurance, love, and a lot of evenings and nights.

You get to see things that many in ministry never get to see. You see transformation, you constantly see new people coming in, and you get to work with people who are incredibly passionate in their faith. The vast majority of people who are Christians begin their walk of faith while they are in their youth. Children and youth workers get to witness much of this with their own eyes.

I am thankful for every person God has called to work with these age groups. There has been a lot of pressure put on these people to successfully deal with the loss of our children and youth from our churches. Along with having to work at camps and retreats, entertain the masses, and pull all-nighters, they are expected to be miracle workers. They are called to do what parents, senior leaders, and churches have failed to do—keep the youth in their church and faith.

Many people in churches all over the world would credit one of these workers with helping them become the person they are today. It is, in part, because there are people like these workers that younger generations exist in our churches at all. I believe these are needed ministries today as we move forward to reach this generation.

## The Staffing Solution Myth Busted

When faced with a decline in an age group, many churches conclude that the best solution is to hire more staff, or more specialized staff, to cater to them. This has enabled many churches to reach out and focus on particular age groups. We hire children's pastors, Junior High pastors, youth pastors, and young adult pastors. While these pastors can be incredibly helpful in our churches, simply having them does not guarantee we will reach and keep this generation.

Before saying more, I need to clarify that these are all valuable ministries. God has called people to work specifically with these age groups. He has gifted many with the desire, patience, and skills needed to minister to both children and youth. I even believe that these ministries are often the healthiest parts of many churches. Because of the success some have had in these ministries, many churches simple copy what others have done and think that those templates must be their solution also.

The idea that hiring professional staff to work with our children and youth means we will retain our youth is false. Consider this: in the last three decades, there has been more youth and youth adult ministry than at any other time in the history of the North American church. This occurred to address a change in culture and ministry as churches reached out to this age group. An incredible number of people were brought into the church through these ministries, and many can attribute their faith to these ministries as well.

At the same time, while we have had the largest increase ever in these specialized ministries, we have also experienced something else—the largest drop-off we have ever seen in these age groups. The myth that the answer is simply hiring staff is completely wrong. The negative statistics on retention even include churches with very active generational ministries. While staff may be a help, the issues over which so many leave the church go much deeper than who is running the programs. So hiring more staff may be the wrong starting point.

In this chapter, we want to speak about all these ministries (children, youth, and young adult), which we will call generational ministries as a whole. If the goal of generational ministry is to bring people into the present churches for the long-term, it has been a colossal failure. In an attempt to fix a minor problem, churches may have inadvertently contributed to one of the largest exoduses in church history.

I do not believe this is due to lack of motivation, or even the methods used by those leading these ministries. Too often, churches have tried fixing the disinterest of the younger generation with Band-Aid solutions without ever examining why they are bleeding in the first place. If we aren't careful, we can have the wrong motivations for operating a generational ministry.

### Are Some Models Anti-Biblical?

Let's look at a few reasons why generational ministry has had failures when it comes to retention. For many churches, generational ministry has replaced God-given responsibility. We very likely have been guilty of creating ministry models and systems that are anti-Biblical. We need to question, *Are our present models working?* If they aren't, there are likely answers in Scripture as to why. We also want to understand what a healthy church needs to do for these age groups.

Generational ministry is not ever meant to be a program of the church. It is to be a *mission* of the church! Many churches do not want to be missional about generational ministry; that's why they hire generational pastors. The church's lack of a missional understanding of generational ministry has to with a misunderstanding of what it means to be a Christian in the first place.

Retention is a direct result of the health of the local church, not of the children's, youth, or young adult ministries. If generational ministries are going to retain young people and integrate them into the church body, they must seek ecclesiological reformation. Churches must understand "church" and "youth and church." Generational ministry is, in fact, the church's ministry. The purposes of the church are the same as the purposes of generational ministry. Generational ministry cannot marginalize young people by simply providing "something for the kids." Many churches have reduced the purpose of running generational ministries to the simple goal of keeping the "real" church free of noise and distractions. This approach has, in fact, worked well for many churches, as they have no one left to bother them.

Today, churches are unhealthy and crippled because they have cut off their own legs, since it will be younger generations who move them into the future. Churches need to bring back the passion and energy of the younger generations into the corporate community and ministry of the church.

### Biblical Parenting

Youth ministry, in many settings, is also expected to replace parenting and our God-given responsibility. While many parents want to blame the state of their young people on the ministers "responsible" for them, much of the retention problem rests on the shoulders of parents. Generational ministries are not meant to be the main spiritual developers of teenagers. The Bible teaches that *parents* are to fill this role. Parent pressure is far more influential than peer pressure in most age groups. However, youth work is still necessary because of parental dysfunction. Unfortunately, there is little or no involvement of parents in most youth ministry models.

Each young person is the product of a unique family system, a system responsible for forming beliefs, values, and actions. If we plan to effectively minister to them over the long haul, we must sincerely desire to minister to entire families. A youth ministry that excludes parents is about as effective as a Band-Aid on a haemorrhage.

According to Biblical pattern, home is the primary teaching institution:

> These commandments that I give you today are to be upon your hearts. Impress them on your children. Talk about them when you sit at home and when you walk along the road, when you lie down and when you get up. (Deuteronomy 6:6–7, NIV)

Too many parents expect the youth ministry to fill this role. Parents have taken a back seat and handed off responsibility to youth workers, whose role should be to support them.

The next chapter of this book will deal specifically with this issue, so more will be said there. However, the point is simple: youth ministry cannot be a replacement of something parents are called to do. Generational ministry must be family ministry. It must equip the family to do what the Bible teaches it to be. Also, generational ministry must be there to help connect young people who do not have a strong Christian influence at home.

### Successful Generational Ministry?

Successful generational ministry is one of the causes of churches not keeping young people as they get older. This statement may seem odd. After all, shouldn't we be seeking good generational ministry? Let's dig a bit deeper.

I believe that the ministry models found in generational ministries are often the most Biblically-based. These ministries are, in fact, places to grow, where questions are expected and discussion happens. They are also places where age-related topics can be discussed on a level which young people can understand.

These are generally places where much grace is extended. It is okay to be different. Community takes place in this setting. Lifelong friendships, mentorship, and discipleship can happen. These ages are taught that our faith cannot just be lived out in a church building. These ministries teach our young people that faith is to be more than a spectator sport. Here, everyone is encouraged and asked to be involved, even though they aren't perfect.

When I was a youth minister, I just didn't preach about helping the poor. I took our youth to work at soup kitchens to give out clothes, talking and ministering to people. I didn't just challenge them to share their faith. We took our youth on mission trips all around the world. We helped them run events where they could share their faith. We taught them to live out their faith by their words and actions.

There was also a social net. If someone was missing, someone noticed. Each individual felt and knew that they had people who were praying for them specifically. They were surrounded by people who were interested in their success and well-being.

So if these incredible strengths exist, why do we see so many of not become active adults in our churches? Well, for the most part, this ministry model does not exist in the "real" church. We have taught our youth to be discontent with just attending church. The philosophy of most generational ministries is not matched by the churches they exist in.

One of the most common questions I'm asked by senior pastors is, "Why won't the youth and young adults become part of the church?" This question demonstrates the real problem. People do not become part of the church when they turn twenty or thirty. If you have not invited them to be part of the church when they entered your doors, they were never really welcomed. After training people for ten or twenty years to think that they are not old or mature or enough to take part in "big" church, why would we suddenly expect them to make the transition?

## The Constants

All of this speaks to a lack of continuity. Generally, generational ministries have failed to implement a long-term multiplication strategy. However, while a generational ministry should have a long-term plan, it must be part of the church's long-term plan. Too often, the goal of youth ministry is to try to get students to adulthood, but just leave them there.

This contributes to the trend of incredibly transient young adults who are searching for churches. They are seeking for something that is missing. They are looking for what they had in their youth or young adult ministry. In time they stop, because most discover it does not exist, or they have no idea how to find it. Young adults will not transition well into the full congregation unless it is as current as the generational ministry they are departing. Much can be said of the shifts in characteristics between the post-modern generation and the preceding modern generation.

I believe many generational ministries would be better described as church plants within an existing church building. The only issue with this is that the majority of people who attend new churches or church plants have almost no interest in attending a traditional church. Once you have been in that setting, the vast majority are completely bored and discontent in a traditional setting. The majority will not transition but will go looking for something similar. Some will find it, some will walk away.

This is partially why I believe there is an incredible shift happening in the Western church today. At one time, organic/non-traditional home churches where a small segment of the larger Christian community, but that is changing. In the coming decades, the number of believers who are meeting in these settings will outnumber those attending traditional churches. This may be a healthy shift. However, it is extremely difficult if you are a traditional church.

This trend is also seen in the incredible drop-off of young adults who have been in various mission programs and campus ministries. Once they return home to traditional churches, the retention rates are dismal. I believe it is because these people have been wrecked for the normal. It is easy shift the blame to these groups, as it is impossible to remain on the mountaintop all the time. However, when was our Christian walk supposed to be considered normal? There is no way for these people to express what they have experienced and how they have grown in an environment that revolves around spectating.

Therefore, many in this generation do not see a connection between attending services and living like Jesus. If you are wondering where this issue came from, it came from us. At a recent meeting, I spoke to over a hundred national youth and young adult leaders. I asked them, "How many of you like going to church?" I could count on one hand how many said yes. My next question was, "Why do you think anyone you lead will attend your church in the future if *you* don't want to be there?"

This is a question we all need to ask ourselves, not just the generational workers. This again shows the incredible shift of philosophy and ministry styles between ministries all working in the same building. They may be close by proximity, but they're miles apart in practice.

For a generation to stay in an existing church, there must be constants. I do not believe the above issue is entirely the fault of generational leaders. Rather it is caused by a church and its leaders as a whole. The philosophies of generational ministries and adult congregations may both be good, right, and effective—at least, on their own. The real issue revolves around whether or not they are working in concert with each other. The problem is caused by wrong thinking and a lack of understanding of what church is.

### Advice

**THE POWER OF STAYING.** Again I will emphasize that one of the keys to keeping a generation is creating constants in their lives. In saying this, we see an obvious problem which has led to another issue of poor retention. Generational pastors are generally very short-term. The average stay for a youth minister in many denominations is eighteen months. Some young people over the course of their time in church have had countless leaders and pastors. It is impossible to grow sustainable, long-term relationships when we think short-term. No depth, meaningful mentorship, or discipleship can happen in short-term relationships. We need long-term workers.

Over the years, I have met several young men and women from a particular church. I have noticed they have an uncommon depth of spiritual health. It didn't me long to discover what many of them attribute their spiritual health to.

Here is the story of one of these young men:

> Don't hate me! Promise? Okay, here we go. I had the same youth pastor (at the same church) for twenty years! Still love me? If that doesn't seem like a big deal, then you most likely are new to the world of student ministry and church life.
>
> I thought having the same youth pastor my whole life was normal. I mean, at age twelve I started attending Shiloh Youth. Then, I started helping at age nineteen, as a single guy. When I got married at age twenty-five, both my wife and I helped my youth pastor as volunteers. At age thirty-two, he told me that I was the new youth pastor (I stress the word "told").
>
> I believe that one person can still make a difference! I also believe that making an impact is rarely attained in one event, or over the short-term. I believe that to really affect lives, you have to spend decades showing up day after day, week after week, year after year, with all the effort, excellence, and love you can offer.
>
> My youth pastor, Bruce Belair did just that for me and thousands of others. Excuse me while I brag on him, but he served as youth pastor of Shiloh Youth for over twenty-three years. He persevered through hurts and

attitudes and offenses—both his own and those aimed at him. He pressed past great victories and achievements where others would have stopped to gloat. He simply loved us, shared his life with us, and preached the Bible every week. His story is a rare one, but it should be a common one.

I know I am where I am today because he just wouldn't give up. So now, as I walk out of my office (his old office), I see a sign I had made that says "Paying it back," which reminds me that change isn't in the sermon or blog; it's achieved in decades of loving God and students.

> – Mike Miller, Shiloh Youth
> www.shilohyouth.ca

There is the power in thinking long-term. Churches need to foster these types of ministers, whether paid or volunteer. It is very obvious that generational pastors are too transient and temporary. Churches must work to entice generational ministers to stay for longer terms. If you are one of these ministers, you need to understand that your effectiveness grows the longer you are in a location.

One must wonder if a local church's generational ministries, in some cases, would be better served (and more people retained) if the generational leaders were congregation members. A congregation member is more likely to stay for a longer duration than present day generational ministers. This is often a very freeing thought for churches who cannot afford a generational worker. Consistency can be more important than apparent giftings.

This also means we need to look at generational ministry differently. Why then are youths considered a separate group from the main congregation? Is church to be only the "home" of generational ministry? Children and teens are the responsibility of the entire congregation, not just youth workers or Sunday school teachers.

Generational ministry must also be positively impacted by the church leadership, and especially the senior pastor. Without an active and continual ministry from the senior pastor, churches can expect to have weak retention. This is due, in part, to the fact that whatever consumes the pastor's heart is also subtly transmitted to the entire congregation. This allows young people greater ease in plunging into the full congregation upon achieving adulthood. (In fact, young people should not feel as though they are entering into the adult church at all; they should already feel a part of the full congregation.)

Adrian Thomas writes:

> There is no doubt that the churches that are significantly impacting young people, which are keeping their youth and also adding young people, demonstrate a deep love and care for young people. In the majority of these churches, the senior pastor and his/her staff have a deep and unconditional love for young people. The young people know they are loved,

> accepted, cared for, appreciated, and supported by the
> senior pastor, the staff, as well as the members of the
> congregation and their families.

This must flow from the top down.

Also, Nigel Cottle says that perhaps we have short-term results because we have short-term goals:

> The reality is that you measure what you value. How
> many youth pastors have "how are the young people
> connecting into the wider church" as a key part of their
> job description and measurements in their reviews?
> The reality is that youth pastors are measured on short-
> term criteria, so that is inevitably what they go for. Pas-
> tors talk about wanting lifelong followers, but that is a
> lofty idea, not something they are measured by.

As pastors, both senior and generational, we must start thinking long-term.

**ADOPT A CHARTER.** Adopt a charter to bless, equip, encourage, prolong, and increase the effectiveness of the ministry of the church. Below is a charter which was developed by a group in the United Kingdom called We Love Our Youth Worker. You can find them at www.weloveouryouthworker.co.uk. Their charter for church youth workers is a set of seven promises churches make about the about the practices and principles they will use in employing a youth worker.

1. *We will pray and support.* We believe that our youth worker needs spiritual support in their work with young people. We promise to pray for our youth worker and keep their needs a high priority in the church's prayer life.

2. *We will give space for retreat and reflection.* We believe that taking time to think and pray is just as essential for our youth worker as organising events and meeting young people. We promise to encourage our youth worker to use part of their schedule to give space for retreat, reflection, and personal development.

3. *We will provide ongoing training and development.* We believe that learning the skills of youth work is an ongoing process and that it's important to continually invest in professional development. We promise to set aside time and money to provide this for our youth worker.

4. *We will give a full day of rest each week.* We believe that taking regular time off helps maintain our youth worker's passion and energy for their work with young people.

We promise to actively encourage our youth worker to take a day away from their role each week to do something different.

5. *We will share responsibility.* We believe that having a youth worker does not release the rest of the church from our responsibilities towards young people. We promise to encourage everyone to play a part in volunteering, praying for, or supporting young people.

6. *We will strive to be an excellent employer.* We believe that it's important to have clear structures and procedures for recruiting and employing a youth worker, and to provide supportive management structures. We promise to follow good practice guidelines in the way we employ our youth worker.

7. *We will celebrate and appreciate.* We believe it's vital to acknowledge what our youth worker is doing and the commitment they have made to work with young people in our church. We promise to make sure our youth worker knows they are appreciated and that we will celebrate their achievements.

**DEVELOP MINISTRY CONSTANTS.** While this may be a new concept to some, I believe it can be hugely effective. The idea is to have people who follow a generation through a church. For example, if a church hired a Junior High leader, he or she would in time become a Senior High leader, then the young adult leader, and so on. This can also be done with adult leaders and sponsors.

Discipleship and mentorship take time. Jesus Himself spent over three years in constant contact with the disciples. Growth takes patience and perseverance. When we think long-term, we can experience stories like the following, which came from a minister who has worked in the above approach:

> "Jeremy." I feel the prod of a boney finger covered in pizza grease snapping me back into my unhappy reality. "Are you okay? You look like you're going to pass out." And maybe I am; it's barely midnight and I'm rethinking my strategy of feeding barely-adolescent boys energy drinks, the crack cocaine of teenagers everywhere. A few forgettable hours later and the post-energy-drink-crash has taken full effect, leaving only a few badly out-of-tune girls at the karaoke machine, and a shrinking crowd at the hockey-fight round-robin tournament. The rest are passed out and having their faces painted with permanent markers.

> "Jeremy." Same boney finger, this time covered in what might have been blood or possibly ketchup chips. "Why are girls so weird?" Good question. Pause. After explaining to him all of the mysteries of the fairer

(and weirder) sex, I can't help but wonder and hope that someday, maybe, I'll get to meet the woman who would eventually fall in love with the grown-up version of this skinny kid, badly in need of deodorant.

Years pass and the greasy pizza nights and conversations are beginning to add up into what my youth ministry books might call discipleship. I'm not really doing much; I pray and then go to his Junior High grad. During high school, I teach him to drive standard while teaching him what it means to pray without ceasing. Eventually, he graduates from Senior High and I give him a high-five and bring him a card. Not one of those five-dollar cards, either—just something simple with a few lines of encouragement and a Bible verse.

"Jeremy." My call display doesn't identify who the caller is, but I answer anyway. "Jeremy, I'm in trouble." It's a sad story of moving away, getting lost and wandering, and finding out some things that he never, ever intended to find out. My heart hurts, but what can I do? I pray, I keep moving forward, I think about him from time to time until one Sunday, there he is! The church has changed; it's grown, there's a new building, I've married off his friends and dedicated their babies—the place is different. Different, but vaguely familiar and he's aware that he has come home to a wide-open and generous welcome. And a life begins to turn.

"Jesus" was all that the subject line of my email read. "Thanks, Jeremy, for walking beside me all of these years and introducing me to Jesus again and again. I just thought you should know that I met a really great girl. She loves Jesus and I think I love her. Can't wait to introduce you to her!"

– Jeremy Postal, Christian Life Community Church
www.clcc.ca, www.jeremypostal.com

**PUTTING OUR BEST FOOT FORWARD.** Here lies one of the issues with generational ministries. We put the people with the least experience onto the front lines. I believe this is the norm, because we think our younger ministers can relate to them better. However, in some cases it shows how little most churches value these ministries and ministers.

While it is never said out loud, there is an underlying thought of, *Let them practice on the youth. When they get enough experience, they can then come and work in real church.* This attitude also contributes to the short stay of many generational workers. The majority are underpaid, undervalued, and have not yet gained the skills and self-confidence to deal with parents, boards, and senior pastors.

What is incredibly sad about this is that the majority of Christians start following Christ in their youth. This is common knowledge to almost all churches, boards, and ministers. If youth is where we will see the most growth, why do we put the most inexperienced people into these positions. If we want to truly invest into our future, should we not be putting our best efforts into reaching and keeping the next generation?

At the same time, many people who use generational ministries as stepping stones to other ministry. Many younger ministers think, *This is what I have to do until I am old enough.* All these mindsets can be dangerous. When we have ministries that are mostly based on hype and charismatic individuals, it will always turn out to be shallow.

As I stated in the introduction, my years of youth ministry never prepared me to raise my own teenagers. In looking back, I can't believe I even gave advice to parents, or that people even listened to me. As I am approaching two decades in ministry, I know I am now more prepared to and equipped to minister in ways that lead to long-term growth. However, few people my age have the opportunity to work with the younger generations. This needs to change. It is time to put our best foot forward.

Young pastors have not had time to develop the skills needed to deal with the pressures and expectations of being a generational pastor. For example, most youth pastors have heard about and know the statistics on retention. Most of them believe that in five years, at least half of those they are ministering to will not be serving God. They also believe it will be their fault. However, this is likely not true.

This responsibility falls to the church, but many feel the weight of expectations brought on internally or by parents, leaders, and pastors. Many will burn out trying, while others will feel like a failure and quit. Only a few will make it. We need to remove this pressure by spreading the responsibility to the whole church, and also by helping them develop a long-term strategy to retain the youth.

## The Purpose of Generational Ministry

We do not do generational ministry to keep the adult services quiet and free from distractions. We do generational ministry to reach people, disciple them, and equip them for ministry. We minister to the young generations to see them grow, to take on the mission of Christ, equip them, and release them.

If we are going to see this generation stay, the church's idea of generational ministry must change. There has to be a shift in our thinking and focus. For example, we consider young people good enough, old enough, and brave enough to go to war for us, fight for us, protect us—and even die for us. However, they are not good enough to walk beside us and lead in the church.

If Jesus' life is our example to follow, we have to question what we are doing as churches. He called together a group of young men. Literally, He called a group of teenagers; perhaps some were in their early twenties, at most. He poured His life into theirs. He walked with them, taught them, laughed and cried with them. He gave all He had for them. This was His example for us to follow. This was the Father's plan for Jesus, and it must be ours also.

Too often, a church's response is to give token ministry to young people, thinking this is involving them. This was not Jesus' approach at all, and it completely fails to bring about the results we want. Jesus sent young people out to share the gospel, cast out demons, heal the sick, and proclaim that the Kingdom of God was at hand. We merely ask them to pass an offering plate.

In the last few years, I have had several experiences which have reshaped my thinking on youth ministry. I had an opportunity to speak to several young people in Columbia who were part of one of the largest youth ministries in the world. There, I spoke to young people half my age who were leading hundreds, and some over a thousand people each.

In Serbia, I met a young man and his wife who were pastoring a Gypsy church. At the age of fifteen, he was reaching into his community and leading this congregation. Stories like this are common all over the world.

In both of these cases, and many others like them, the common factor is that someone believed they could do it. Someone released them, sent them, and covered them with blessing. Is this how we view the younger generations in our churches? Do we believe God can do this for them? Are we willing to release them, or do we ask them to wait their turn?

If as a church we can equip and release our youth and young adults in the gifts God has given them, we will take hold of a great future.

The issue of retention related to generational ministry really rests with the older generation—not the younger.

There are, in fact, much deeper issues that need to be addressed apart from whether or not we're relevant, trendy, and cool enough to attract people. There is something we need to allow God to do in us first. There needs to be a turning point in our spirits. We need to see our young people in their potential. We need to let the heart of the Father turn to the children once again.

Jake Kircher, a youth pastor and writer, wrote:

> Church and youth ministry leaders often throw quotes around like, "Teenagers are the future leaders of the church if we only wait," but when push comes to shove, their involvement can often take a backseat to the "professional" youth worker. When we do this, we damage teens' understanding of the theology of church.
>
> The New Testament church was about people, not a building or organization. Every person was involved and gifted, as Paul explains in Romans 12 and 1 Corinthians 12, and no one should be left out. Church is not something we should be doing or going to; instead, the church is something that we as followers of Christ need to be. God reaches people with people.
>
> For far too long, we have communicated to our students that they are not needed or that we don't have a place for them in leadership. We have told them to

wait until they are better versed in the Bible, the guitar, or public speaking. We have created programs and events that don't center around allowing students to lead, and instead we focus on ourselves, the bands we hire, the great speakers we bring in. Our students have a ton of fun, but at the same time, many have learned that ministry and church should be left to the adults.

This is the exact opposite of what Jesus intended. The "professionals" of the time—the Pharisees, the Sadducees, the priests, and other religious leaders—were overlooked as leaders for this new lifestyle. Almost every interaction Jesus had with them was one of challenge and rebuke. They were totally missing the point with their religion and their understanding of the law.

Instead, Jesus turned to a group of misfits and used them in such a powerful way that it turned the world upside-down. Jesus was making the statement that a relationship with Christ is not about the experts, the professionals, or those on top of the social hierarchy. But it *is* about those willing to be used by him.

Today, there is a lot of conversation about where the 18- to 30-year-old demographic has gone in our churches. I think one of the answers to this question rests on what we have taught them about what the church is and what it means to be part of the church. We in youth ministry have an important responsibility to think critically about what our programs and structures are teaching kids about this issue.

Though we mean well, are we being more like the Pharisees and religious leaders and sending the wrong message? Or are we being like Jesus and helping teens to *be* the church and have a powerful impact on their communities?

– Jake Kircher
www.jakekircher.com

## Advice

**FOR PARENTS.** Ask how you can help with the generational ministries of your church. Get involved. There will be many children and youth who need to see a Godly parent and family in action.

Tell your children's and youth leaders that you are sorry for putting all the responsibility of bringing up your kids spiritually on them. Let them know you will be trying your best to do your part and will also be praying for them.

**FOR GENERATIONAL WORKERS.** If you are presently involved with running a generational ministry, ask yourself, "How much of my time is directed towards equipping parents?" On your calendar, start planning a few events a year just for parents. Even if only a few take part, you need to know this will have more lasting effect than many other things you do.

Get over yourself. You are not the number one spiritual influence in the lives of all those you lead, nor are you supposed to be. If you are trying to be, you are not leading in disobedience to scripture.

**FOR SENIOR PASTORS.** You need to decide on some practical steps you can take to ensure your generational leaders remain in your church.

Have your leadership discuss whether or not your church structure is actually inclusive to all generations. Do you have a long-term strategy to develop your young people into leaders in your church? If not, it is time to start developing a plan which includes all the staff and ministries of the church.

We asked Marcel deRegt, the leadership development director of Youth Unlimited, to answer the following questions:

What are a few things a church and its generational leaders do to develop a retention plan?

- Have open and often communication between church leadership and youth worker.

- Have clear guidelines to the role of the youth worker.

- Always support each other in public, regardless of personal feelings or decisions made.

- A youth worker can't do it all. Find their strength in ministry and build on that strength.

What can a church do to support and work with its youth leaders?

- Respect their time in and out of the office.

- Make sure budgets are there to send them to conferences and retreats.

- Help them in their ministry; walk alongside them.

- Do not expect them to be the "saviour" of youth ministry in your church.

- Provide them with the resources they need.

- Develop a good prayer support team.

## How can we equip youth leaders to think long-term?

- Pay them well.

- Do *not* view youth ministry as a stepping stone to greater things.

- Provide them with the training and sole care needed to avoid burnout.

- Focus less on the programmatic side of ministry but on the relational aspect of ministry.

# The Family

03

# The Family

# 03

We will not hide these truths from our children;
>  we will tell the next generation
>  about the glorious deeds of the Lord,
>  about his power and his mighty wonders.

For he issued his laws to Jacob;
>  he gave his instructions to Israel.
>  He commanded our ancestors
>  to teach them to their children,

so the next generation might know them—
>  even the children not yet born—
>  and they in turn will teach their own children.

> So each generation should set its hope anew on God,
>
> not forgetting his glorious miracles
>
> and obeying his commands.
>
> – Psalm 78:4–7

## The Power of Family

There is nothing my wife and I want more than our own children to succeed. They are our greatest joy, and at times they are also our biggest worry and stress. As our children are now all either teenagers or young adults, we are still trying to figure out the balances of time, influences, trust, and all the right things we should be doing as parents. By the time we have it figured out, they will likely all be moved out. However, we can then practice on our grandkids.

If I want to see those I lead to succeed, whether they be my own children or people God has brought into our lives, it will mean a lot of work—and sometimes pain. I have discovered that if I truly want to make a difference in this present generation, something needs to start in my heart before I can begin making strategies and plans. God needs to turn our hearts towards this generation.

In Psalm 78, we read about what the end result will be when we pour ourselves out for our children—*"So each generation should set its hope anew on God"* (Psalm 78:7). We also learn about what needs to happen, what we as parents have been instructed to do, what we have been commanded to do. Through scripture, we have been instructed to pass on what we have to our offspring.

As a Christian, I believe God has given us responsibilities for two distinct groups of people. One, of course, is our immediate families. As parents, we have a responsibility to care for our children. We need to nurture them, provide for them, protect them, and we need to pass on to them everything God has given us. Our immediate families are our first responsibilities.

We also have a larger family of other believers. These people should be so dear to us that the entire world knows we are followers of Jesus through the love we have for each other. The Bible gives us some very clear commands of what we are to do for this family. We are to pray for them, pick them up when they fall, encourage them, spur them on to good works, and meet together with them.

The next chapter will deal with this group specifically. This chapter, however, is focused on your children, as the reader, which likely means you have some church connection or faith yourself. However, it is very obvious that a large number of children and youth do not have a strong Christian influence in their families. They may even be from a family that discourages it. However, every young person needs what is written about in this chapter.

Our own misunderstanding of the power of family has led to many leaving the church and their faith. We do not understand our roles and responsibilities as parents, pastors, and leaders. Neither do we understand what effects they truly can have on others. It is even possible that some of our own church models are detrimental to the spiritual formations of our own children—including our spiritual children.

The number one reason people give for returning to their church and faith after they have left for a season is the influence of family. While I am sure the work of the Holy Spirit plays a huge part, family is what the majority attribute their return to. We cannot discount the power of family. It is the reason so many began their walk of faith and the reason why so many return. At the same time, it is also the reason that so many leave.

## Fight for Your Family

The one thing we can do that will affect our future the most is simply investing in our families. We need families to take up their God-given duties and responsibilities. We also need to fight against manmade systems, which take away our God-given responsibilities. You cannot let anyone, even a church, rob you of what God has given you to do.

We have been trained to treat our children's spiritual upbringing like their secular education. We send them to a school so that other people can teach them. We then send them to college, where again they learn from others. We send them to Sunday school, to youth group, and hope that someone else is making sure they turn out okay. Many Christian parents are not involved in the spiritual upbringing of their children at all.

I am not saying that you shouldn't send your children and youth to Sunday school, youth group, or some Bible class or club. However, these things should only be supplements to the Christian environment they are in seven days a week. Simply sending your children to someone else for teaching does not bring about long-term growth and retention. It is the combination of classroom teaching, seeing real life examples in their family and friends, and being part of something larger (the church) that brings about spiritual health.

In fact, the spiritual upbringing of our children needs to be a priority. We often let this be secondary to the other involvements our children are involved with. More often than not, we have more interest in making sure our children are involved with sports before they are involved with activities to grow them spiritually. Parents need to go out of their way to make sure their kids are involved in spiritual activities to the best of their ability.

Adrian Thomas is a church and pastor equipper in the Dominican Republic. He says:

> Even here in the Dominican Republic, many of the over three hundred pastors we work with are concerned about the lack of youth in their churches, as well as the flood of young people leaving the church to never return. They have tried many different suggestions, ideas, and programs, yet it seems to have done little to stop the trend. In the midst of all this, there are a number of churches that are not only keeping their youth, but young people are flocking to

them. Using these churches as examples, I would like to suggest some things we all can consider that may help to keep our youth in church no matter where we may live.

One thing that has a direct influence on keeping young people in church has been the priority families have placed on being involved in the spiritual lives of their children. Most of the parents are actively involved in the spiritual lives of their children in and out of the church. As well, the churches teach that the parent has been commanded by God (see Deuteronomy 6:4–9) to bring up their child in the ways of God, and it is one of their primary responsibilities. The churches prioritize teaching and preaching on family, and the God-given responsibilities of parents and children. Parents are taught that they must make it a priority to discuss spiritual things through family devotions and prayer, and be more than willing to give spiritual guidance to the issues and concerns their children face as they grow up.

If you visit these churches, you will also see parents demonstrating a passion and love for God and the church. They are actively involved in the life of the church, passionately worship God, and listen and respond to God's Word. Their children see parents who love God, love the church, and are not ashamed to demonstrate their love for Him in worship and in response to God's Word. Outside of church, the parents, in the midst of economic struggles and their own personal daily struggles, try to exemplify and live out a life that resonates with faith, hope, and love for God and His Word. There is no doubt that this has an impact on their children as they see their parents modeling a life where the church is important, and God and His Word impact and influence them daily.

– Adrian Thomas, Dominican Republic

www.everydayministries.com

## Splitting the Family

I believe in age-appropriate ministry. Because of their distinct nature, younger generations need specialized attention. There are certainly age-related topics that are not applicable to everyone. This cannot, however, lead to the total segregation and isolation of some age groups. It is true many churches are set up in a way that a family never attends, worship, learns, or ministers together.

Families show up to a building together, but they often head off in all different age-segmented areas. Teens head to their service, children go to children's church, and the adults go to the sanctuary. If family is the most important spiritual bond and influence we have, then some church structures are detrimental to long-term spiritual health.

Do not think for a moment that this only refers to Sunday services. In our Christian walk, it is important that we talk, worship, and minister together. However, we are limiting ourselves if we only think about how to accomplish this in a sixty- to ninety-minute segment of time per week.

This segregation can lead to our younger generations not feeling a part of the church family. It is conceivable that some people have grown up in our churches and have had no contact with the larger gatherings of the church except for special occasions.

Complete segregation also hinders young adults from eventually stepping into leadership roles. A thirty-year-old may have incredible leadership skill, and have ministered in generational ministries for years. However, the adult body of the church has never seen them and doesn't really know who they are. Many of these people, as they come out of the generational ministries in which they were very active, are now simply overlooked for leadership. These are not people who will ever be content just attending services, but that is all they will be asked to do.

Total segregation makes for settings that are free from distractions. It helps to have quiet times with God. It helps us to be focused on learning and worship. These are all needed and important things at times. However, if our goal is that everything be like this, we are hurting families and our future.

## Connecting the Dots

There is a huge disconnect between the beliefs of Christianity and the practices of it. For example, in Canada, most people believe in God. Not only do the majority believe in God, but they believe in

Jesus. However, only a small fraction is living out a relationship with God.

In our churches, there is also a disconnect between what we believe and the understanding of what church involvement has to do with those beliefs. In fact it seems the more people want to live out their faith, the more trapped they feel in a church setting, where the majority of time is spent spectating.

We need to connect our beliefs to our practice. There are some easy ways to do this. This is one of the arenas where family and smaller ministries can really invest. As we raise our children (both naturally and spiritually), we need to let them understand that there are things we do because we are Christians. While this can include going to services, it must go beyond that into everyday practice. A simple example is saying grace. We do this because we are thankful. Let your children know that it is not simply a tradition; rather, teach them that you want the act of saying grace to express thanks to the God who provides. We need to live out our reasons for doing what we do.

Too often, our young people only connect our Christianity to negatives. They are told that because we are Christians we don't drink, we don't smoke, and we don't sleep around. We need to let our youth understand that there are things we do, as Christians, that are right, true, just, and helpful to society. Help connect the dots.

Our children need to see us doing things for God because we are Christians. It can be the giving of our time, our generosity, our words, or so many other examples. Our hope is that our children see the sacrifices we make for them and our community, and then connect it to our faith.

## The Spiritual Role of Parents

There are things that we are called to do for our children. First, we need to understand as parents and believers that we are not simply called to produce offspring. In fact, everyone, or most people, have the desire and ability to procreate. However, not everyone wants to be a parent and take on the responsibilities that come with that. Through experience, we have all learned that parenting has some of the biggest joys and upsets all mixed together.

As believers, we need to make the connection that part of the great commission is a call to spiritual parenting. You and I are called to make disciples. Our first lifelong disciples are, in fact, our children. Just as Jesus called His disciples to follow him, we have to take on the responsibility to lead spiritually. Our children will follow and learn from our example. We need to be what we want our children to be.

It is not enough to tell children to go to church, be involved, or have a strong spiritual life. Your example will be a greater influence than your verbal instruction. Your passion to make sure they are getting fed spiritually in your home, at church, and at events should be obvious.

## Moving Past Procreation

One of the reasons we have low retention and such shallow faith in our churches is that many people do not want the responsibility of parenting spiritually. We have given away this responsibility, commission, and hope someone else. We have wanted to do our part in conception, but we haven't assumed the role of spiritual leader.

> " The church I go to isn't a family. Its members don't know each other and there are few opportunities to get to know each other, if any. A spirit of division prevails, inciting judgment, criticism, and gossip. "

Parenting goes beyond just producing offspring. In fact, we can produce offspring without taking on the role of a father or mother. Spiritual parenting moves us much deeper and carries much more weight. We are not called to just produce children. Indeed, we are not called to just raise children.

As a parent, I am not simply called to produce and raise my sons and daughters. Spiritual parenting means we are called to raise future fathers and mothers. This role moves us into a place where we understand that our role is to raise up men and women of God. As a father, my sons need to learn what it means to be a good husband, a provider, a spiritual leader, a father, and a man of God. Spiritual parenting involves us discipling our own children to become mature Christian parents and leaders.

## The Cost of Success

One of the more difficult statements that Jesus made was that if we want to be His disciples, we must be willing to take up our cross and follow Him. There is certainly a price to pay to follow Him, and there is a price to disciple and parent others. Discipleship and spiritual parenting certainly involve a cross, and death. They involve us putting aside our own desires, needs, and plans. In fact, we must be willing to die to ourselves.

Our motivations, purposes, and thinking change when we become parents. Our focus shifts from ourselves to the new ones now living in our homes. To bring long-term change, we need parents to come to a point where they are comfortable that part of their success will be found in the success of their children.

> **"**
> In the original churches in Acts, they broke bread together, shared scripture together, and were one in spirit and purpose. If we let come in and out of a church gathering, or anything that we do that represents the body of Christ (even our friendships), and we don't treat others like family in love and truth, why would anyone want to stay? We're to love others so that they will know we are his disciples!
> **"**

Just as in discipleship, a parent's true success can be seen when their child becomes a good father or mother.

When Jesus gave instruction on fruitfulness, He told His disciples, *"I appointed you to go and produce lasting fruit"* (John 15:16). As spiritual parents, our goal cannot be to simply be fruitful, but to be fruitful and multiply. Until we focus on raising fathers and mothers, we are only being fruitful. When we invest in the future, we move into multiplication because the line does not end, but grows. I believe this is one of the reasons that throughout the Bible God is mentioned so many times as the God of three generations.

Many times in scripture God is referred to as "the God of Abraham, Isaac, and Jacob." Three generations has to be part of our understanding of what we have been called to as parents. For too long, parents and the church have been very short-sighted. Our success cannot simply be judged by whether or not there is a second generation, but rather if there is a third. The influence of fatherhood and motherhood spans three generations and beyond. The God of three generations is also called Father. The influence of Godly parents spans from generation to generation. By the Father's example, we need to reach our influence past one generation.

### Slowing Down to Get Farther

For most of my life, I have been involved with various extreme sports. If there is something I love, it is to go fast. Whether it has been mountain biking, snowboarding, or four-wheeling, there is a personal enjoyment in going fast. This has led to a few injuries in my life, but I wouldn't take them back. However, as I have gotten older, it seems I take fewer risks. We do gain some wisdom as we age.

Sometimes we learn more in a moment than through months of reading, classes, or sessions. Last winter, I had one of those unexpected moments where God spoke something into my life through my own children.

My youngest, Amanda, decided that it was time she learned how to snowboard. I had been taking her older brothers for years and now she wanted to join in. What you need to know, though, is that snowboarding has been a passion of mine for twenty years. I started skateboarding when I was seventeen. Then, two years later, I started snowboarding and I've never quit. There are few things as enjoyable in life, to me, as carving down a mountain at high speeds. I think I was made to go fast.

If there is something that drives me crazy, it is going slow. When I come up behind a car going below the speed limit, I admit to wondering, *What is wrong with this person?* I was never made to stay still. I even find the thought of working in a church and maintaining what is already there a bit offensive.

The first five days I took Amanda snowboarding were painful. For her, because she kept falling, and for me, because I never got to snowboard. I was *on* one, but I never once got to go fast. I never once enjoyed the speed. Instead, every ten feet I would pick her up, give her some instructions, a push, and wait for her to fall again.

On this particular day, I was sitting in the snow waiting for Amanda to catch up. We were on the trail right beside the snowboard park. I was watching different young people go over the jumps and sliding on the rails. As I was watching, my middle son Jordan came through the crowd, went over a jump, and was gone from view as quickly as he had come. He was going fast.

It was in this moment that a realization of deep truth hit me. There were other years when I hadn't gotten the chance to go fast—the years when I was teaching my boys how to snowboard. Now here I was sitting on a hill, seeing Jordan fly by me just as fast as I could go. Today we all get to the bottom in a reasonable amount of time, only falling occasionally. Today we can all go fast. If I had never slowed down, though, I would have been the only one going fast. I would get to the bottom, but I would be all alone, with my children watching from the sidelines.

## Surpassing Us

As good parents, we want our children to succeed in everything they do. However, our desire for them must go even further than that. As we invest in our children, our goal should be that they actually surpass us. A good father is not threatened by the success of his children, but desires it. Parents should want their children to go further. Our prayer should be that this generation receives a double anointing of what we are walking in.

If our goal as believers is to see the world hear the gospel, then we have to be surpassed. For a worldwide transformation to happen, our children are going to have to see and experience something that we have never seen before. My sons, daughter, and disciples will have to walk in a different kind of way than I ever did. It will mean that those coming after us will have to surpass us. We cannot truly want worldwide transformation if we cannot desire to be surpassed.

## Walking Under Our Blessing

Our children need to walk under the blessings of their parents. In the Old Testament, we see incredible examples of the power of blessing that comes from a parent. Fathers would lay hands on their children and their words would speak into their future generation. It seems that the lives of young people, their directions and destinies, were changed by the blessings given by their parents.

Speaking blessings go way beyond just saying positive things to our children. Speaking blessings, however, is also extremely important. In the natural, we know that words can have a dramatic effect on a person. Our words have the power to destroy. As believers, we are to build each other up, encouraging and serving one another. How much more should we be doing that for those closest to us? There are so many people who have a negative view of Father God because of the relationship they had with a parent. Our words need to be an example of Christlikeness, filled with grace and truth.

There are also spiritual principles at work. As stated, blessing flows from parents to their children. I am extremely fortunate that I grew up with parents who did this for myself and my siblings. I remember hearing my father say publicly and privately that his prayer for us was that we would go places in ministry he never did, that we would be used by God in ways he never was.

Just as my parents spoke blessings over me, I now also pray and speak blessings over my own children. I am certain that part of who I am who and where I am today is because of the upbringing, prayers, and blessings passed on to me by my father and mother. I now pray that my own children—Matthew, Jordan, and Amanda—will be blessed. I pray that every good thing God has given and imparted to me will rest on them in double proportion. I pray that they would experience things in God that I never have, that they would go further, believe for greater things, and that the world would be a different place because they serve God. Speak blessings over your children.

### Persistent Prayer

There are times when we can do all the right things as leaders and parents and it seems everything still goes wrong. I have seen incredible parents whose children have been deeply challenged. I have also seen young people who strive in their faith whose parents are far from being good examples. We need to understand that we are dealing with people who have the ability to make decisions for themselves.

Parents who have children far away from God may be carrying both sadness and guilt. The truth, however, is that everyone needs to decide to follow God for themselves. It is never too late to reach out. It is never too late to encourage, to be an example. It is definitely not too late to pray.

Looking back on my own youth, I know that I caused my parents quite a bit of grief. But there is something about having parents who don't give up, who stay up praying when their kids don't come home, who don't let go when their kids choose to run away, who stand looking and waiting for their lost son to return.

I have never been without a home, without a family, without someone to call out to when I was in trouble. I have always known that someone believed in me. I have always known that someone was calling out to God on my behalf. We need to be persistent in prayer, love, and grace.

Pastor Carey Nieuwhof, when asked if he could give some advice for parents, wrote the following:

> I remember the first day of kindergarten for both of my sons like it was yesterday. How quickly things change! My youngest just entered high school and my eldest has gone off to college. Gulp.

Some of you are gulping, too… your eldest is in kindergarten (you can hardly believe it as you say this to yourself)… your youngest just started his final year in elementary school… your toddler is speaking in complete sentences. I know… it's hard to believe. I promise you, it never gets easy to believe. It just happens.

If there is one phrase that can sum up what I've learned as my children have grown up, it's this: You have less time than you think and more influence than you realize.

I think most parents mix up these two things. We think we have more time than we do, and we have less influence than we actually possess. But the difference is critical. Think this through for a moment.

You have less time than you think.

- I've never met a parent who was sending their kids to college or into the marketplace who said, "This took far too long… I'm so glad I don't have more years with them." It flies by for all of us. So while you've got the time, leverage it. Don't wish it away. Don't take it for granted. Pray about it. Above all, make the most of it. It won't last forever.

But you have more influence than you realize.

- All the studies say the same thing: at every age (including the teenage years), a parent has more influence over a child than peers, media, teachers, friends, or any other influence. So even though yours kids might be getting older, your influence continues to run strong.

In light of this, it becomes critical for parents to leverage their time and influence. Here are some ways you can do that:

- Widen the Circle: Pursue strategic relationships for your kids. Work intentionally with your church, with other adults, and with peers who can be a positive influence in the spiritual and character formation of your child.

- Imagine the End: You do have less time than you think and more influence than you realize, so focus your priorities on what matters most.

- Fight for the Heart: Whatever you do, don't give up on the relationship you have with your son or daughter. Fight for them, not with them, by communicating in a way that gives your relationship with them value.

- Create a Rhythm: Increase the quantity of quality time you spend with your children. Your church can help by giving you resources to use in your time with your kids over the course of a week.

- Make it Personal: Your kids are watching to see if your faith is authentic. It's okay to put yourself first when it comes to personal growth.

If you and a wider circle of influence of church leaders and other adults partner together, you can make a critical impact on your son or daughter with the time and influence God has given you.

– Carey Nieuwhof

www.careynieuwhof.com

www.orangeparents.org

Jonathan Lambe, a key youth worker in Bermuda gives this advice to parents and youth workers:

It seems like raising teenagers for many parents has become a war where allies and enemies have become a blurred distinction. Many parents and teenagers have been the victims of friendly fire, because the best of intentions have been perceived by the recipient as a deliberate violation and/or an all-out attack. How do genuine allies turn into the worst of enemies? Is it just a phase that all teenagers go through? Is it that parents just don't understand?

I daresay it's none of it and all of it at that the same time. Every generation had to battle the previous generation for their own identity. In your day, it might not have been hip hop, but rock and roll. It might not have been pants sagging so the underwear was showing, but it might have been crazy hairstyles or dog collars worn as jewellery. Each generation fights for their own identity.

I would like to offer my two cents on how to remain an ally with your children. As we grow older, we grow wiser (hopefully) and understand just how powerful free will is. I think all of us wish we could go back in time to stop ourselves from some of the choices we made, and yet it's those choices that have made us into the people we are today. We want to shield our children and young people from making the same mistakes we made, and yet we don't want to disclose the reasons why we are telling them "no." So our children look at us like we are so out of touch. They think what they are doing, or are about to do, is "new" or so original that there is no way we could understand their choice—and the friendly fire begins. Here is some advice.

1. Do *not* destroy their dreams. I don't care how crazy it may sound. Unless their dream is going to put them in immediate danger or a near-death experience, do not kill it! If they are sharing their dreams with you, this is an invitation into their life, their identity (at the time). Embrace it, and try to understand it. If you attack their dream, in their mind you are attacking them and you just lost their trust and have officially become their opponent.

2. Embrace their dreams. Be supportive and show interest. If they have truly become passionate about a dream or vision in their life, you can use that as leverage to steer them in the right direction and curtail negative

behaviour. When someone becomes passionate about something, they will do things they don't want to so that they can do the thing they love.

3.  Ask God to give you the courage to share your real testimony with your kids and to help you take advantage of every teaching moment, while gently guiding them into the perfect will of God for *their* life. Do not be afraid of your kids' dreams. They may not be your dreams, but that's okay.

– Jonathan Lambe
www.reignlive.com

## Love and Time

There will be many influences in the lives of your children. As spiritual leaders, we need to make sure we are positive ones. My prayer is that my own children will look back on their time with us and be able to say that their father and mother loved and served God, but also that we loved them.

One of the most precious resources and gifts we can give our children is our time. We cannot mentor, speak into the lives of our children, or teach them anything without being with them. One of the ways they will know how much they are valued by you is by the amount of time you spend with them. Go out of your way to find chunks of time to spend with your children. Talk to them. Answer their questions. Play.

We want to raise our own children to make the right choices for themselves. Of course, this is never guaranteed, as some people can only learn by their own mistakes and victories. I believe this happens as a result of the things addressed in this chapter. As we are examples, as we model Christ, as we encourage, as we answer the tough "why" questions, we are teaching them to follow God and make the right choices.

In the end, everything revolves around us making our children know the love of God and the love we have for them. This needs to be the motivation behind everything else we do. Go out of your way to let your children know they are loved, that you are proud of them. These are our most precious gifts; let's make sure they know it.

## Advice

**FOR PARENTS.** Write letters and notes to your children, even as teenagers and young adults. Let them know that you are proud of them and their accomplishments. Tell them they are loved.

As a family, sponsor a child. Let your children pick who they are sponsoring. Make them a part of the process. Also, make sure to use this as a lesson about how God's heart leans towards the poor. Teach through the process how we are to love, care, and help our neighbours, as this is a huge part of what it means to follow Christ.

Visit Kiva.org and find a person to help start a small business in the world. This is an incredible organization which is helping to stir up local people to fight poverty around the world. Again, do this as a family. This type of experience can be used every few months and can be a great way to bless others as a family.

**FOR PARENTS AND LEADERS.** Go on mission trips. Many churches are involved with doing mission work around the world. It is quite common for these to be age-centered. However, I believe it is incredibly powerful to let families minister together. It is an opportunity for parents to work alongside their children.

Closer to home, you can visit and work at a soup kitchen or do some kind of outreach together. This does not have to be something you do on a weekly basis, but parents should attempt to do ministry with their family at least a few times a year. These experiences are priceless. Churches and generational leaders should incorporate a few of these types of events into their schedules.

# The Power
of Adoption

04

# The Power
# of Adoption

# 04

I have been given all authority in heaven and on earth.
Therefore, go and make disciples of all the nations,
baptizing them in the name of the Father and the Son
and the Holy Spirit. Teach these new disciples to obey
all the commands I have given you. And be sure of
this: I am with you always, even to the end of the age.

– Matthew 28:18–20

## A Generation of Orphans

When one person enters into the Kingdom of God,
even heaven stops and takes notice. When we see a
person giving their lives to Christ, whether it's for

the first time or a prodigal is returning, we also rejoice. This is a time for celebration.

As incredible as this is, our goal as parents, churches, and ministries cannot be to simply win converts. If our primary focus is on spiritual birth, we are producing something I refer as the "Orphan Generation." This is a generation which has been birthed but has no one to care for it, to feed it, to teach it, and to be its family.

If a baby is left on its own, it will die. In many of our modern evangelism events or crusades, we see that only a very small percentage of those who accept Christ are actually now living a Christian life a year later. Many churches and ministries will boast of their huge success, but without real follow-up and doing what the Bible has instructed, it is, for the most part, very short-lived and highly ineffective.

We have more tools at our disposal than ever before to share the gospel with the masses. We have television, radio, print, bigger buildings, crusades, sound systems, and now the internet. We have more ways of scattering seed than any other time in history, but we seem to have less seed falling on soil that produces long-term growth. The idea that we are to produce converts, and not disciples, has to be broken.

Discipleship and real follow-up have been the weakness of the modern church. Even though our vision and mission statements likely include something about discipling our community and world, it is rarely seen. We are guilty of looking for instant results without demonstrating any real commitment on our part. Much of this falls on two possible causes. First, a vast majority of churches have become places you attend to solely hear teaching and worship. These are valuable parts of what we do as believers, but we are called to be so much more. Our church models and practices have taught people that this is what Christian living looks like.

A more disturbing truth is that we do not want to do discipleship. Doing this would mean taking on the responsibility of discipleship and parenting our new believers. We would have to change what we do. It is not all about us.

At the deepest level, there is a lack of understanding of what it means to follow Christ. He called His disciples to follow Him, to do what He did. Just as He taught them, they were to now teach others. This is a Biblical principle that many who call themselves Christians do not want to embrace. It is messy, it is work, and it involves us.

We have also been found guilty of giving away this commission and responsibility to others. Whether it be the pastor, a small group leaders, or a teacher, the bulk of the work seems to fall on a few people. In the back of our minds, we are just hoping that somehow it will all work out, or that someone else will take care of it. However, no matter what the cause, too many "orphans" are left to die.

The younger generations in our churches may come from many different types of backgrounds. Some of them may have strong Christian parents, others mays not. Some have some church background, while others do not. A vast majority of believers, though, will not have family. If no one takes a personal interest in these people, an incredibly small percent will stay. We need to adopt.

> For even if you had ten thousand others to teach you about Christ, you have only one spiritual father. For I became your father in Christ Jesus when I preached the Good News to you. (1 Corinthians 4:15)

## Adoption

If our desire is to see a generation stay, we have to be willing to open up our lives to the family of God. Spiritual adoption means that we invite new and young believers not only to our church programs, but also into our lives. As Paul became the spiritual father of Timothy, we need to follow His example and do the same for those around us.

For this to happen, something must change in how we view this generation. All churches want growth, youth, and a future. They do not, however, want everything that is going to come with that. Churches are sometimes upset when they get what they prayed and worked for. Children are noisy, messy, a lot of work, immature, and more than we bargained for at times. Unless our hearts change, we will never let them become family. We need to first be willing to adopt.

It is not just an invitation to become part of a church or the family of God. It is an invitation to become part of your family. The questions we need to ask ourselves are:

- Am I willing to let the spirit of adoption work in my life, ministry, and church?

- Am I ready to let people see the real me?

- Am I ready to love and serve those God puts in my path?

- Am I really ready to adopt new family members?

It may sound incredibly simplistic, but if we do not adopt the next generation, they will not stay. It is a sign we have not truly welcomed them to be a part of our churches. It is also a sign that we have become self-serving institutions. When a church's heart changes and a spirit of adoption prevails, its motivations change. It takes us past just hoping we have young people attending our services to us having sons and daughters. Just like our own children, there is nothing we should desire more than to see them succeed.

## A New Old Discipleship

As followers of Christ, we are certainly called to make disciples. This is not just the ministry of a church, it is your personal ministry. It is the ministry of every believer in the church. While we recognize the different giftings God entrusts each one of us with, discipleship is a calling that reaches everyone in some way.

Being Christlike means living like Christ. To take on His characteristics, His love, His compassion, and so on. However, we cannot be truly Christlike if we are discipling no one.

We can be guilty of picking what parts of Christlikeness we want. We can say we want patience, we want to be merciful, we want to love more… well, these are certainly all parts of what the picture of Christlikeness is. I believe that doing what Jesus did is also part of Christlikeness, as His actions flowed from who He is. You cannot be Christlike but not want to do what He did. He made disciples.

Do not fall for many of the misconceptions about discipleship that have gripped many. Discipleship does not take place just because people attend church programs. Discipleship does not just happen. Discipleship is not just for new Christians. An entire church cannot be discipled by a single minister.

In Colossians, we see what our goal in discipleship should be:

> Then the way you live will always honor and please the Lord, and your lives will produce every kind of good fruit. All the while, you will grow as you learn to know God better and better. (Colossians 1:10)

It is our calling to become more Christlike—to live in a way that honours God, to produce fruit, and in the process to get to know God even more. This is what we should want for ourselves and those around us.

Discipleship starts when someone is called to follow another person, just as Jesus called His disciples. There is a connection between those involved. It includes adoption. It involves becoming spiritual mothers and fathers. Discipleship is spiritual parenting.

Discipleship involves people coming into our lives. It involves us having new family.

A common misconception is that discipleship happens when we attend church. This misconception includes the thought that a minister has the ability to disciple an entire congregation. Both thoughts are incorrect and bear little fruit. In scripture, the crowds were called crowds. The disciples were called the disciples. Churches and ministers, often pridefully, call the crowds disciples. The Biblical model, though, would prove us wrong. We can't disciple crowds like Jesus discipled His disciples. It is simply impossible, always fails, and is not what Jesus modeled for us.

### Why Is Discipleship So Important?

Consider this. In the beginning of Acts, there is an event that took place in what we call "the upper room." One hundred and twenty people were represented there. Have you ever wondered who they were? We know who some of them were. The remaining eleven disciples, likely many of the seventy-two disciples, and many others who would have been close to Jesus.

At this point in history, things have dramatically changed. Just a short time earlier, huge crowds were following Jesus. Thousands would come to hear Him, to see this man who some thought was the Messiah. However, there was now a price to pay for being associated with Jesus. There was danger involved.

When the going gets tough, it is those who are discipled who stay. Those who are closest remain—the people who have been poured into the most, the ones who saw and heard personally, those who were involved with ministry. Discipleship produces long-term growth, not short-term converts.

It seems like Jesus was never looking for a great mass of people. At times He would intentionally do things that would chase people away with difficult teaching. It seemed His focus was on a few people. It was about discipling and modeling something that would last, something that would spread, something that would reach the world.

## Jesus' Model

Much of my teaching and writing rests on this simple belief: Jesus modeled for us what discipleship looks like. He modeled God's plan to take the gospel to the entire world.

As mentioned in the last chapter, here's what Jesus modeled. He found a bunch of young men, all in their teens and perhaps a few in their early twenties—at the most. He poured His life into them. He gave them His time. He gave His instruction and teaching. He showed them what following the Father looked like. He equipped them. He sent them out. Everything the Father gave to Him, He gave to them.

He even called His disciples friends. How different is this from most ministry models today? There is the clergy, laity, leaders, and many classes. Do we in leadership call those we lead friends? Are they really our friends? To disciple like Jesus, those you are pouring into must be.

The following experiment should be the litmus test for you to know whether you are actually discipling people. If everyone on this planet was asked who they were following, would anyone say your name? If anyone in your church was asked this question, would anyone say your name? If not, you have not adopted anyone.

That may sound extreme, yet it is the Biblical example we have. Paul said, *"And you should imitate me, just as I imitate Christ"* (1 Corinthians 11:1) Also, if anyone asked any of the twelve who they were following, clearly they would have said Jesus, as He was their Rabbi. However, I also believe if you asked Jesus who His disciples were, He knew, as He had called them to follow Him.

There should never be one young person, young adult, or anyone in any church who has not been adopted by someone, or a group of people. A huge majority of people who have kept their faith would testify that they had this type of relationship with someone. Everyone should have someone who is praying for them specifically, someone who is pouring their lives into them, someone like Paul was to Timothy, like Jesus was to the twelve. Everyone needs someone who loves and cares for them individually. There should never be an orphan in our midst.

There is a huge lesson to be learned here. If we are going to reach and change the world, we need our youth and young adults to be involved in the work. Much of the modern church has become ineffective because its people have not released this generation. A church's ability to grow and live out its purpose rests in the passion of its youth. This is who Jesus called. Why would we try something different? A church is truly healthy when we realize that we are a body of many parts—not just one generation. A church without children is stagnant, passionless, lacking wisdom and direction. We feel momentum when we are all working together.

Don Mann, the founder of Reinventing the Church, has done research on how Christian Bible college/seminary students feel about the church, and what they are looking for from us. His conclusion needs to be a challenge to us.

> Recently I had the privilege of spending an afternoon with the entire student body of Summit Pacific College in beautiful British Columbia. My task, given to me by the denominational leadership the college is a part of, was to lead this group of next generation leaders into a discussion on the present and future effectiveness of the church.
>
> The results of this discussion speak for themselves. What you are about to read should cause all of us who presently lead the church to wake up to what the generation coming behind us is thinking. We have formed our opinions based on how they look, talk and act, without taking time to listen to their hearts. It is time that we stop and listen before they say goodbye and leave the church completely!

Here is what they had to say when given the opportunity to speak without the risk of being judged.

- Less focus on pleasing congregants and more on what God wants—love people where they are at and not where the church *wants* them to be.

- The current culture doesn't want the "mega church" mentality anymore—recognize that we are not defined by our buildings—be missional.

- Get back into the Bible—reverse Bible illiteracy. Too focused on the clock—don't be afraid of the Spirit.

- Altar calls—allow for the Spirit to move.

- Re-evaluate the relevance of traditions—do they foster growth in the community or cause division, are they open to change or do they hinder change?

- We must maintain a cross generation connection (mentorship).

- Next Gen needs to feel empowered—they want to sense that our input is valued.

- Give the next generation a chance—don't be scared we will take your job—we want your knowledge, wisdom and experience—listen to what we have to say because we know our generation—it would be good to be heard.

- Allow us to take risks—don't let us tip the scales too far—we need balance and need to be accountable for what balance is.

These final comments speak for themselves. Are we willing to listen?

"Please mentor us, invest in us, give us opportunity—listen to our hearts—don't judge from our outside appearance. My generation needs *you* to step up to the plate and invest personally in our lives; otherwise who can we learn from?"

– Don Mann, World Traveller
www.reinventingthechurch.com

## Sons Go Further

In the last chapter, we discussed how parents long for their children to succeed and even surpass them. When the spirit of adoption begins to grow in a church, that same premise should apply. A church desire the success of our younger generation and new believers. When they truly become part of our families, our thoughts and dreams for them change.

Our success needs to be found in the success of these people. As leaders, our success needs to be found in those we lead and not just in our own abilities or thoughts of greatness. The truth is that our sons and daughters go further than us. This generation will not be released in many churches, simply because they are not their children. Matthew 10:24 says, *"Students are not greater than their teacher, and slaves are not greater than their master."* However, if they are our children, we want them to surpass us. We are in a losing battle as long as we either have an "orphaning" mentality or simply think of ourselves as teachers and not parents.

It is here where we can understand that the concept of three generations applies not only to our immediate family, but to our whole Christian family. A church will only experience long-term growth when it lays down its life to reach, invest, disciple, and parent its own young. In other words, when it does what Jesus did for the disciples.

David Wells, who gives leadership to the Pentecostal Assemblies of Canada, writes the following advice:

> Lifeway Research, in one of their extensive studies of young adults aged 18–30, identified several characteristics that seem to help predict if a young adult will drop out or continue attending church. They are:
>
> - Teens wanting the church to help guide their decisions in everyday life.
>
> - Teens who, at age seventeen, have parents who are still married to each other and are both attending church.
>
> - Teens who find their pastors' sermons relevant to their life.
>
> - Teens who have had at least one adult from church make a significant investment in them personally and spiritually between the ages of 15–18.

It does not take rocket science to figure out the core factors that encourage youth and young adults to stay engaged in the life of the church. Put a young person in a context with a holy combination of catalytic persons (both parental and adult examples), relevant church experiences, and a personal motivation to participate in a meaningful walk of faith, and the majority will be active in a visible faith community.

No guarantees, but if you want your church to have engaged youth and young adults, ensure that:

- The worship and equipping life of the church is substantive and applicable to real life.

- The role of the family in discipleship is honoured and equipped.

- The contexts for youth and young adults to be influenced by mature followers of Jesus are intentionally in place (formal and informal).

- Life-appropriate spiritual formation is the lead activity, with other events (social/recreational) being complementary.

– David Wells
www.paoc.org

## Working Together

At first, the issue of working together may seem like a concept that is difficult to implement. And it is almost impossible to implement if our only connection is a service which takes place once a week. While churches are good at doing corporate worship and sermons together, they are not always set up to connect people in mentorship or coaching relationships. Doing so must be intentional.

One of the biggest influences that determines whether a new and younger generation can feel welcome or part of a church is the senior minister. They can be even more of an influence than even the generational workers. The direction, vision, and heart of a church usually flow from this person. Therefore, his or her heart needs to be focused on reaching and investing in our sons and daughters.

Churches and ministries must do all that they can to foster mentorship, discipleship, and adoption. In looking at the ministries your church provides, there must be some which bring together people of different generations. It must be more than simply attending a spectator-based service together.

There are some easy and practical ways to do this. First, do ministry together. It is possible to do the ministry of the church as whole instead of it being limited to one generation. For example, the men's ministry and youth group could take on a work project together. Several generations of the church could go on a mission trip. All ages can help at a soup kitchen a few times a year. Small group or home groups can be done geographically, instead of being divided by age groups.

Also, when we think of the ministries in our church buildings, we need to have all the age groups involved. The younger generation will learn to minister, pray, and equip others as they watch and minister with us.

Too often, our ministry positions are given to people with obvious skills and leadership abilities. We often give them to those who have been believers for a long period of time. However, one of the true signs of Christian maturity is that it has the ability to reproduce itself. One of the prerequisites for ministry is that its leader be willing to pass on what they have to others; they can't just do all the ministry on their own.

When we begin to think of mentoring and discipling others, one of the biggest issues that comes up is time. It takes work and time. However, there is something extremely easy you can do. Look at what you have in your life now. What interests do you have? What do you spend time doing? What ministries are you working in? Once you have thought of a few things, determine not to do at least one of these things alone. This can be something very simple—a sport, a hobby, a Bible study, playing music, etc. Connections are developed in these times spent together.

While these are just a few ideas, there are many more. Our goal should be to have ways where people can connect naturally. As we become family as a church, these things should happen by themselves. We are to be known for our love for one another, including those new and younger. If we love them, we will do all we can to adopt and keep them.

Ashley Beaudin, a young writer from Canada, wrote the following thoughts:

> The other day, I was waiting outside the movie theatre and heard a conversation in passing. Two women, both around sixty-five years of age, were exchanging thoughts. One says with delight, "Kids, eh?" to which the second woman responds, "We were them once." This simple statement began to echo through my heart. It's easy to forget this. Everyone gets old… it's inevitable. Many once stood where I now stand— a young person in pursuit of God. Many now stand where I will one day stand—a person rich in wisdom and faith. But many of us across this spectrum lack the intimate experience of having true relational community with each other.
>
> It was during my first year of university, after talking with my social movement professor, that I realized the church is one of the only places where generations ever cross paths. Despite this, due to our culture, you will notice that the generations are compartmentalized even within our churches. I believe God wants the church to be a point of convergence for the generations. I believe He wants us to forsake our worldly culture and adopt a heavenly culture, declaring that we are the family of God—we are one.
>
> Before life with Jesus, I was a little girl stuck in the middle of a family that was falling apart. I watched divorce lay siege on our family, creating instability and

fear. Infidelity, abuse, and lies laced our home and our relationships. I knew about Jesus. But my life felt dark and I was pretty sure He couldn't do anything about it, so I didn't care. I had yet to realize how much He really did care.

I will never forget the night I gave my heart to the Lord. I don't think any of us ever forget the experience of realizing that God is who He says He is. I wasn't saved because of persuasive words or because I was evangelized. I wasn't saved because we played really good games at youth group or because someone prayed for me at the altar. I gave my heart to the Lord as I sat on my bed in my room. He came and met me, and I was changed.

The Lord began to transform my world. I started to view life as an adventure with my Father. Wow, I had a Father in heaven who loved me! That was power. I wanted to walk by faith and live out my dreams, with an understanding that anything can be conquered because my God did the impossible. He turned me into a young woman of confidence. I am under a system of grace, eternally loved and made to love. This was the power that set me free.

Soon I came to a point in my walk with God where, even though I experienced the Lord and His beautiful promises powerfully, I needed a family. I needed a spiritual family. I needed mothers, fathers, brothers, and sisters. This became my plea before the Lord. Friends, can I share something with you? There is a cry in my generation. We are hungry for spiritual family. Many of us come from broken homes. Many of us haven't been properly fathered, and we don't know what authentic family looks like. Because of this, our souls crave it. We go to church and have no connection or mentorship from the older generation. We don't hear from them, and rarely do we find ourselves serving alongside them. This deepens our cry.

We dream of a church that is a spiritual family—a family that walks in intergenerational ministry. We want to be mothered and fathered, nurtured and protected. Sit us down and tell us the truth straight up. Society tells us lies all day long. We need the truth, and we need to hear it from you.

Without spiritual family, we're disempowered. We don't feel confident in our identities, giftings, or callings. We backslide and fall away because we're in pursuit of love and radically devoted relationship, the kind the church was made for. When we can't find it among our family, we settle for the cheap stuff. But friends, when we do have spiritual family—we walk in destiny. We learn to be who God wired us to be. We know that at the end of the day we can come back to our Papa, who loves us, and our family, who cheers us on.

My hope is that more youth will find opportunities for this to become a reality in their own lives... opportunities for the generations to seek God together,

> minister together, grow together, and connect with
> one another in meaningful ways. I have experienced
> this to some degree and know how satisfying it can be.
>
> – Ashley Beaudin
> www.ashleybeaudin.com

On her blog, Sarah Cunningham, who is the author of *Dear Church: Letters from a Disillusioned Generation*, wrote the following words, entitled "How to Search for Family." I think this is an important first step we need to take.

> Step 1: Take a reflective look at the people in your sur-
> roundings.
>
> Step 2: Search complete.
>
> Sure, the people around you may not have grandma's
> trademark dimpled chin or Uncle Elmer's pointy, mis-
> shapen ears (thank God), but from a faith perspective,
> we all may be more connected than we think.
>
> Three questions for consideration:
>
> 1. Does the person look like you or any of
>    your relatives? Well, they have to, right?
>    After all, we all look a little like our maker
>    (Genesis 1:27).
>
> 2. Is the person related by blood? Absolutely.
>    God brought us all together through the
>    blood of Jesus (Colossians 1:20).

3.   Do you have a parent in common? Totally.
We have the same Father (Romans 8:17).

If we look a little alike, we're related by blood, and we
have the same Father, I think it's okay for us to act a
little more like family. Don't you?

Pass it on: we're family.[1]

## Advice

**FOR PARENTS.** Try to get your children into mentorship relationships with strong believers who are older than your children. I am
so thankful that my own children have a few people they really
look up to who are strong Christians. If need be, go search for
these people.

**FOR GENERATIONAL WORKERS.** Set up prayer partners with
other groups in the church. For example, you can have the seniors
group praying for the children in Sunday school by name. This
will create a place where everyone is being prayed for. It will also
forge connections and bonds between the young and old.

**FOR MINISTERS.** Make sure you have a way to identify those who
have no Christian home influence. In these cases, the church body

and leaders really do need to adopt these people. As stated, the
percentage of young people who remain in church who do not
gain these types of relationships is close to zero.

---

1    Sarah Cunningham: Crowdsourcing Life. "How to Search for Family." Accessed: February 23, 2011 (www.sarahcunningham.org).

# The Hypocrites Craziness, and Pedophiles

**05**

← **Departure**

# The Hypocrites, Craziness, and Pedophiles

## 05

There are many reasons why some people leave their churches, and others leave their faith altogether. They may not even be able to always give you an exact reason, because their exit was never planned. They may have just slowly lost interest as their life became filled with other things.

There are those who have rejected the gospel for various reasons, which we will discuss in the upcoming chapters. They may have a problem with the concept of God in general, or perhaps even the God of the Bible. They may have left still believing, but not wanting to live it out. In a sense, they are living in rebellion, knowing the consequences yet choosing to live in sin.

There is another group, though, that has left because of what they have seen and experienced in the church. These people are living with the results, hurt, pain, and memories of things that should never have been done. There is no doubt about it. There are people who will never set foot inside a church again because of the words or actions of another person. There are those who want nothing to do with God because of the shortcomings or abuse of someone who was, or pretended to be, a believer.

When a wrong is done in the church setting, it is so destructive, because we have been told that the church is a safe place. It is in the arms of the church, we find acceptance, mercy, and compassion. We are family. People let their guard down. We trust. This is the last place we expect the evil of abuse, gossip, manipulation, control, anger, and sin. Yet it comes in waves sometimes, and many are destroyed in the wake.

### What Now?

"We don't know what to do. We can't go back there," a young couple once told me. While I am not Roman Catholic, I do work with many people who are, as I live in an area which is predominantly Catholic. The young couple I was meeting with was about to have their first child. While it may not be the same as your theology, they were torn about having their baby baptized. According to their beliefs, not having this done meant they would be risking their child not going to heaven. However, to have their baby baptized they would have to go to a place they said they would never return.

What could be so bad that they weren't sure what to do, even though they believed this could have eternal consequences for their family? In their church setting, they had witnessed repeated offenses of physical and sexual abuse by clergy. Just weeks before this conversation, another church leader who they had great respect for had been arrested on very disturbing charges. Now this young family, while holding onto some belief, was at a point where they were unsure if they wanted to be part of the church, its leaders, and perhaps their very faith. In their eyes, all their trust and credibility of the church had been completely destroyed.

Whether we like it or not, the actions of churchgoers affect the perceptions people have of the entire church—and of God. The abuse and hurt caused by family, church leaders, and clergy become roadblocks to God in the minds of so many. Even the church's response to its own sins, or lack thereof, have left distrust, anger, and hopelessness in the hearts of both victims and observers.

In the end, we have to ask ourselves, how do we protect ourselves, our children, and every generation from this? There are no simple answers. As long as there are people involved, there is guaranteed to be failure and evil among us. However, we need to do our part to ensure that what people see in the church is Christ and nothing else.

This is one lesson we need to take seriously. We need to pray and ask God if there is anything we are doing as individuals, ministries, or churches that is putting up roadblocks to God, or causing people to stumble, that He would correct us. We have to remember that God is our Heavenly Father. He is also God of the younger generation. When we do something that can hurt one of them, we are messing with family, with His sons and daughters. We have this warning:

> "
> I guess it started when I was sixteen. I started feeling like church was really fake... like everyone was just trying to out-Christian each other. I got tired of all the hypocrites in my youth group, I got tired of being judged for the tiniest infraction, I got tired of praise and worship just being a big concert for all the musicians and singers to showcase their talent... I don't know. It all just felt like a big show.
> "

But if you cause one of these little ones who trusts in me to fall into sin, it would be better for you to have a large millstone tied around your neck and be drowned in the depths of the sea. (Matthew 18:6)

## Evil Has Certainly Been Done

Often we don't know what to do with the evils that have been done in the name of God, or by those bearing His name. Our first step, though, is quite simple. Admit them. We are living in a new day when nothing is hidden. What happens in a small corner of the world can be broadcast around the world in a second. We cannot hide our own pasts, our own wrongs, and we must not pretend that we can.

> **"** I can't go back. I have definitely gone too far. The church has hurt me and my family. I am definitely trying to get over it, but every time I try, anger rises up so deep that I curse them. **"**

There are many present day evils which are being done, but there are also issues people have with Christianity because of its history. Whether it be witch hunts, the crusades, slavery, or the treatment of women, we have things in our past which simply should never have happened. While some people may admire Jesus as a great man or prophet, they have issues with what has been done in His name throughout history. The actions of His followers have clouded the image many have of Him.

All of these things are being used as reasons that our youth should not be Christians. If you do a quick scan of the material being used by groups dedicated to destroying the faith of young believers, their ammunition almost always includes our own history. The reason being, if this is what people who follow Jesus do, why on earth would you be a Christian? Christians have killed thousands, priests continue to sodomize children, they picket funerals of troops who die protecting us, they even hate each other… and the list goes on. Why would you want to be a Christian if this is what history continually shows and proves them to be?

When I look at these things myself, I am embarrassed, saddened, and wish things were different. Our history has become part of the reason for why many people in the world, even those raised in the church, believe that we would be better off without religion, and perhaps even God. It seems that so much of our present day conflicts and world suffering revolves around religion.

### Where Is the Love?

Much of what drives the younger generation out our doors is much closer to home than even our own history, however. It is what people see and experience themselves that seems to affect them the most. It is difficult to even explain, and impossible to justify, why believers hurt one another. It is a paradox how the church can be Christ's body and yet it hurts and destroys its own.

When our children and youth experience churches that are full of fighting, splitting, control, and gossip, they begin to question if anything there is real. When the adults and leaders have said one thing but are obviously living and acting out another, it confirms to our youth that the gospel does not work. It plants the seeds of doubt. It shatters their innocence. It shows them that churches really are full of hypocrites. We have to ask ourselves, how do we prepare our youth to deal with what the church is called to be versus what their church experience currently is? Some may, in fact, have had great experiences, but for many it has been the opposite.

## Starting Points

If you want to gain someone's trust, there is no better way than through honesty and transparency. We need to come to terms with our own history, acknowledge our failings, ask for forgiveness, and then move on. As stated, we cannot hide history or the truth. This includes church history in general, but also what has happened in local churches. Everyone knows of the giant elephants in the room, even when we try to ignore them.

Nothing brings people back together and facilitates healing like when we humbly ask for forgiveness. When there is a move towards acknowledgement and reconciliation, all the hurt, resentment, and mistrust starts to fade. As leaders and parents, we need to model this in our homes and churches. When we are wronged, what is our first response? To turn the other cheek or lash out? To be angry or forgive? To listen or shout?

Christians fail. As much as we do not want to admit this, it happens. Perhaps in our striving for holiness, Christlikeness, or position in our churches, we have lost the ability to acknowledge our own failings. Our structures and church models don't always allow any kind of weakness. They do not even offer a place where we can *"confess [our] sins to each other and pray for each other so that [we] may be healed"* (James 5:16). But there are many lessons we can learn through this scripture. First, we know that leaders will be judged. There is certainly a responsibility that comes with God's calling.

At the same time, we need to acknowledge that even those we preach about and read about in the Bible, those who were even used to write scripture,

> "
> It's strange that the more I learn about the man who gave the Sermon on the Mount, the more I am repulsed by born again Christians. It's not because church leaders are human and make their own mistakes (often very public ones). It's the people filling the pews that really disgust me. The people who picket mosques. The people who vocally oppose gay rights. The anti-abortionists who offer no compassion, and no solutions beyond condemnation. The soccer moms who treat the church like their personal clique... Those people scare the heck out of me!
> "

made mistakes. It would even seem that many, if not most, of the Bible characters had flaws. God seemed to choose the weak, the unexpected, the unlikely, and those who were rejected to do His work. God never chose them because they were perfect. The message is still the same today: *"But God showed his great love for us by sending Christ to die for us while we were still sinners"* (Romans 5:8)

While we are on a journey to become more like Him, we have to admit that we are not yet perfect. This is not lowering the standard, as we need to keep our eyes firmly fixed on Jesus. It is acknowledging that as long as we are on this side of heaven, we will fail, we will sin, and we will let people down. We must acknowledge that churches are full of hurting and messed-up people. We are all in process. While we are indeed growing in Christ together, we aren't there yet.

Taking ourselves off our pedestals means we have to admit our own humanity and need for Christ. We are not super-Christians. We don't repel every attack from the enemy. We are a group of people who are trying our best to live under His grace and mercy. Be honest about the struggles you face. The perception we have created about ourselves is the reason people are so shocked to out to find out about our personal failures within the church. This perception says, "Everything here is free of the failings of man." However, it is not.

If you go on Youtube, you can watching the "fails" of people trying just about anything. There are people falling, crashing, and humiliating themselves. In our churches, there are lots of examples of "fails." You can read about them in newspapers, hear about them on the radio, watch them on TV, and find countless examples on the internet. These are testimonies of where life has taken even those who at some point were trying their best to follow God.

One of the ways to combat this is to give good reports. Our testimonies are powerful. They bring encouragement, hope, and proof that the gospel does, in fact, change us. When life seems to surround us with the discouragement that failure brings, we need to hear the voice of hope. We can become overwhelmed with bad reports, but we have to realize that they are only a small portion compared to the amazing things happening in our communities and around the world. Make sure these good reports are being heard. These far outweigh the negatives.

In the end, leaders and parents have a responsibility to protect those they are raising. If a church is abusive or toxic, a family would be better off to leave and find a healthy place to worship and grow than to lose their children to bitterness and resentment. We also protect by not falling into certain traps. For example, what you do as a parent will speak more powerfully than even the wrong actions of others.

In Matthew, we read the instruction Jesus gave His young disciples: *"I am sending you out as sheep among wolves. So be as shrewd as snakes and harmless as doves"* (Matthew 10:16). This also need to be our goal. We need to live in freedom, not bound by the hurts caused by others. At the same time, we need the wisdom and discernment to stay away from destructive people and situations.

What do we do if the damage has already been done? Many of us will deal with people either on the verge of leaving or who have already gone because of the reasons mentioned here. I believe there is chance for us to gently restore them. We have the opportunity to listen to their stories and empathize with their situations.

While trust may have been broken because of past situations, this is your opportunity to rebuild that. Agree that some situations are wrong. Stand up for what is right. We need to let people see that the church is much bigger than one particular place and person. We need to help people come to a place where they can forgive and walk in freedom again. This process may take some time, patience, and your friendship.

### Painting a New Picture of Jesus

Christianity certainly seems to be struggling with an image problem. Simply ask a few people what they think of Christians and you may get more information than you want to know. Have you ever wondered where this has come from? How on earth did we get such a reputation?

For a people who follow a God who said, *"Your love for one another will prove to the world that you are my disciples"* (John 13:35), we are certainly known for other things first!

What is even more disturbing than to know what the world thinks of us is that these perceptions are almost identical to those held by the younger generation. While outsiders may say we are intolerant, judgmental, out of touch, irrelevant, or hypocritical, so do our own. In fact, we are embarrassed of ourselves. How many conversations have you had, or heard, which include disassociating from other Christians. Statements like "Yes, I am a Christian, but I am not religious" are common. Or perhaps, "I am not much of churchgoer, but I consider myself a Christ follower." We have to invent new terms to describe ourselves because we are tired of being immediately stereotyped.

> "
> There are many reasons that I left the church, reasons which are way too complicated to explain, but to sum it up in one word—hypocrisy. This does not mean that I have lost my faith in God, but that I have lost all faith in the church and what it stands for!
> "

The reason why perceptions in both groups, the church and unchurched, are the same is because they are rooted in the same sources. First, there is a spiritual side. If the devil can make the church seem irrelevant, people's eyes will be blinded to the truth. Seeing as most people come to know God in their youth, this is the war zone. There is a spiritual battle we must be aware of. We need to be strong in prayer, keeping this generation covered.

The other root cause is us. We are the cause of our own image problem, and it is not going to get any easier. It can be uncomfortable to see how Christians are portrayed on television, movies, or other forms of media. However, it is downright embarrassing to see the way these so-called Christian act.

We are living in a day when any person, no matter what their beliefs or ideas, can speak and let the world hear about them. Those with something constructive to say and those with something negative have equal voices, equal ability to spread their thoughts. A quick look on the internet will show you the extent of the problem.

Those who call themselves Christians have messages of hate. They spend their time and resources solely on destroying ministries different than theirs. They show the world how much they are *not* known for their love for one another. In an attempt to speak truth, many have even used wrong mediums, like the internet, to bring correction instead of doing what scripture commands and going directly to the person they have the problem with. The world is the audience to the freak show called Christianity.

Ask a young person in your church what they think of most Christian television, televangelists, or Christian personalities. For the most part, they do not want to be associated with them. If they are honest, many do not want to be associated with our churches at all.

As a leader, parent, or minister, you have to ask yourself, *What are we known for?* What is your family known for? What is your ministry known for? What is your church known for? If your top answer isn't "People who are passionate for God, demonstrating love for each other and their communities," something needs to change.

People will remain in communities they want to be a part of. If your youth, or any age group, wants to be disassociated, in time they will leave. We are in an age where people really want to see the purpose of their involvement. It is important to give this generation a chance to let the church be known for the things the Bible says it is to be known for.

In essence, we need to paint a new picture of Jesus. Remove the one which has been tarnished by the past. Look into scripture and help people live out what believers are called to do. If we truly are created to do good works, then release people to do good works. If your church is known for being self-serving, then it is time to serve radically. Perceptions can change.

This happens when we involve people in painting this picture. Seeing Christ in action trumps any argument someone can bring against Him. Seeing Christ at work through your own hands shows us how real and ever-present the Holy Spirit is in our lives. Make opportunities. Your church and ministries should be involved with something which this generation wants to tell their friends about. It is time to overcome evil with good. If we did this, it would be embarrassing for others to talk badly about us, because our communities would see the good we do.

Start painting.

## Advice

FOR EVERYONE. Pray for your pastor or minister at every meal. Doing so demonstrates honour. It is hard to talk badly about the people you are praying for. We need to cover them in prayer, as we do not want them to fail.

# I can't Live Up to This

# I can't Live Up to This

# 06

**Failing**

There are many things I can't do. Some I can't do because I have never tried. Like skydiving, for instance. Some things I can't do because I am just not good at them. Like golf. I prefer not to even go to a golf course rather than embarrass myself. There are also things I can't do because I have never tried hard enough. Like the playing the piano. I know where middle C is, but I know I will never play a song without a lot practice and dedication.

Despite trying incredibly hard, I could not learn or master the French language. I grew up in a bilingual province in Canada where both the French and English languages are spoken. However, our family moved to a different province, where only English was spoken, when I was twelve. Several years later, I decided to take French as a course in high school. I thought this would be an easy subject, since I remembered at least hearing French spoken when I was younger.

I was greatly mistaken. Halfway through my first semester, I was failing. For the rest of the year, I went for extra help two lunch periods a week, as I had never failed anything before and I wasn't about to start now. However, despite the honest effort, things did not improve. Perhaps I should have known better; it took me several years longer than most people to learn my own language! I struggled with a speech impediment when I was young. I was rewarded for all my hard work and extra time with an absolutely incredible final mark of nineteen. Not nineteen out of twenty, but nineteen out of a hundred. I couldn't do it. I really, really, really failed.

We need God to open our eyes to see what is causing people to miss out on everything God has for them. Several years ago, I was sharing at a young adult event with a few hundred eighteen- to thirty-years-olds. The vast majority of those attending had either grown up in the church or had been involved for quite a while. During a prayer time, I asked how many of them had or were battling the thought that they were a "Christian Failure." That night, almost every person present raised their hands to say, "Yes. That's me."

I had explained that a "Christian Failure" was someone who has repeatedly and sincerely tried to live for Christ, but seems to keep falling or failing. They may have had many experiences with God. They may have been born into the faith. They may have spent many honest years seeking after God. Yet despite all these things, they keep ending up in a place that feels so far from God.

This is a person who, no matter how hard they try, feels that they are a failure to themselves, and most importantly to God. There are many in this group who even come to the conclusion that while Christianity may work for some people, it won't work for them. They think, *Maybe it will work for my parents, and the older people in my church.* Because of their experience, they start to believe that they cannot be a Christian. They may even conclude that either something is wrong with them, or God just doesn't work the same way for them.

No matter what the cause is, failure brings many things with it—disappointment, feelings of low self-worth, guilt, and depression. No one wants these things to rule their lives, and most people will do whatever they can to get out of it. For many, the way out is the back door of their church.

### I Am a Failure

Since that night, I have begun to understand how much of an issue this really is. Over and over, I have heard stories of people fighting this battle. They are broken inside, battling self-worth, wondering why God doesn't care for and love them. They may be miserable, as their Christian experience has been filled with everything other than the joy and life they have been promised. The only feeling they associate with their church is guilt.

> "
> The church, as we see it, is to be a gathering of people where we can stand up and say we are wretched, and everyone will nod and agree and then remind us that we are also beautiful...
> "

The Bible clearly teaches that the Holy Spirit will convict the world of its sin. However, we also know what Romans 8:1 says: *"So now there is no condemnation for those who belong to Christ Jesus."* While most people may have that verse in their heads, it has not moved into their hearts, and with it a proper understanding of how God works.

These thoughts and feelings of condemnation and failure are not from God. Conviction of sin is. However, the majority of people dealing with this issue are the ones who are attempting to follow God and not those who are walking in rebellion. For some, these thoughts have their root in their upbringing. For others, it has come from incorrect teaching. Much of it is also based on insecurity, fear, and comparison. We have a generation of young people who have felt like they could never measure up to those around them in the church. To them, it may seem that they have been asked join a faith that makes life more difficult. In a sense, they feel that they have been set free only to become slaves again.

"
What bothers me most about "church" is that you can't be real. There is no forum for those who doubt yet are sincerely searching. There is no place where you can just be and allow yourself to walk through whatever path you are on; there is always a path catered for you and everyone around you, and don't step out of it. There is no room for differing opinions or even nuances in theology, because how would we keep the order?
"

The severity of this battle means that the majority of those who leave really don't want to come back. Most of the people who have fought and lost this fight now claim that they are much happier since they gave up trying. They have no intention or desire to return to the pain they are now free of. Some of those you live with, and are leading, are dealing with this very issue right now. We need to examine a few ways we can speak truth over the lies people have believed.

## Beautiful Diversity

There are no two people exactly alike. God shows His incredible creativity even in the endless diversity of His most prized possessions. We have different personalities, interests, body types, colors, and dialects. Just as mankind is diverse, so is the body of Christ. It has many different parts but is only truly alive when it is all together.

Growing up is enough of a challenge for most youth. They are trying to find where they fit, discovering their own self-worth and identity. They are surrounded by many messages that can make them feel like they are not good enough, cool enough, skinny enough, or good-looking enough.

There are also some unique challenges for children and youth who grow up in the church. Some of our youth will fit in and make connections naturally. At the same time, it seems like some just can't seem to find their place as easily.

> "
> We have not allowed room for mistakes in the Christian walk. We have been judgmental when Christians screw up. On the flip side of that, when we have screwed up we haven't admitted our mistakes. We have hidden to cover them up. We haven't apologized when we were wrong.
> "

We are called to equip this generation for ministry and the work of the church. It is certainly possible, though, that we portray a very narrow view of ministry which excludes many. For example, if someone is a gifted public speaker, a musician, or a great singer, they can find a place rather quickly. However, if they are not gifted in those areas, they could easily think there is not a ministry for them. There are young people who have felt like second-class citizens. They are wondering why didn't God create them like those who have a "higher" calling.

We must be sure that we do not create or model a caste system in our churches and ministries, one where a certain gifting or part of the body is elevated over the others. This always leads to people comparing themselves to others. Someone is always left out. They can feel like something is wrong with them or that God just doesn't love them as much as the gifted people. They can feel like failures.

One of the most freeing statements a young person can hear is, "It is okay to be you." A person's self-worth is not to be found in how they compare to another person, but rather in Christ. This may be a beginning point to help those who don't feel they are a piece of the body know they are actually an important part.

In 1 Corinthians, we read, *"But our bodies have many parts, and God has put each part just where he wants it. How strange a body would be if it had only one part!"* (1 Corinthians 12:18–19). We need to let the younger generation know that God made them who they are for a reason. There may be people who will only be reached and hear the gospel through the unique gifts and talents He has put into their lives. Even though the verse says how strange it would be if we were all the same, this is exactly what many ministries strive for. It can't be. God give the gifts. He has made us each how He wants. Diversity is His plan. Fighting it and longing for conformity means we are fighting God and being destructive to the body of Christ.

## Advice

**FOR PARENTS.** Take an interest in the talents, abilities, and hobbies of your children. Encourage them to use whatever gifts God has put in their lives for Him. This will build an understanding that the everyday things are part of the gifts God has given us. It also teaches them that ministry happens everywhere, not just inside a building at a particular time.

**FOR LEADERS AND MINISTERS.** Release and equip people to minister with the gifts God has given them. Let people try to reach their friends and circles of influence. Teach on the diversity in the body of Christ. Through diversity, we can reach a diverse community. We need to celebrate and release those who are different than us.

In your events, encourage creativity. Do not fall into the same routines. Let gifts other than music and speaking be seen and heard.

Showcase people, both youth and adults, who have been able to use the things God has put into their lives for Him. This can be sports, arts, careers, etc. Let your groups hear how these are used for worshiping God.

## What Is Wrong with Me?

Comparison will always lead to feelings of failure, as there will always be someone better. Not only can people compare their spiritual and natural giftings to another person, they can also compare their spiritual experiences. When people hear a testimony of a "God experience" or a kind of miracle, some may begin to wonder, *Why won't God do that for me?*

This is very common when we, not just younger people, are faced with difficulties or tragedy. I was recently in a service where a young man named Rob was sharing. Several years ago, he was diagnosed with an inoperable brain tumour and given just days to live. Through a series of miraculous events, he is alive and well today, cancer-free. This is an amazing story of how God still works today. I love these stories. In the same service were several family members who had just lost one of their own to cancer.

While I know testimonies build up faith, I know they can raise a lot of questions for people living through similar situations. Why didn't God do the same for them? Was someone else more important to God than they were, or their family and friends? Did they do something wrong?

There is another way that people wonder if they are a failure or have something wrong with them. It is not just a matter of why God won't do the same for them, but why doesn't He do that *through* them? In the book *Goodbye Generation*, I shared how I even wondered what was wrong with me personally. I have read the gospel accounts and seen the miracles that Jesus performed. In my lifetime, I have heard so many testimonies of the amazing things God is doing today.

I have even read about miracles in scripture that took place with just regular people. Miracles like when Peter's shadow passed over a person and they were healed. While you may not have ever tried this, I have walked by the lame, crippled, and sick. I have done this on sunny days when I was casting a shadow. My shadow appears to be broken, as I have never seen someone jump up healed as I walked by.

So why doesn't it work? There may be several reasons for that. However, how does a young person interpret why? Is there something wrong with them? Perhaps they have done something wrong. If they come to the conclusion that the problem is not them, they turn to another idea—that it doesn't work at all.

> **"**
> I have felt like giving up. Many times. I actually *did* give up one time. At that time, I did not want to be a Christian anymore, although I was afraid that I would burn in hell. But His love was greater than my disappointment. He turned me around. The thing that did it was the realization that I could not change myself to God's liking, or His standards; therefore, I just had to trust in what He promised. I trust that He will not remember my sin.
> **"**

## The Cross and Grace

These are likely just a few of the pitfalls some of our youth face as they navigate through their teen and young adult years. It may be hard to comprehend how something that is called "The Good New'" can seem like such a burden. It was never meant to be.

I do have some advice for people who feel like failures, for those who feel like they can never measure up to God. This advice for everyone who has tried over and over but seems to keep falling into the same trap. It may seem like strange advice at first, but it works. Here it is: *Give up and stop trying.*

Many people are still trying to earn their salvation. They can't. They are fighting a battle that is impossible to win. It is a battle they were never intended to fight. This is why people who say they are happier since they quit trying may be telling the truth.

The truth is that, indeed, you have failed. In fact, everyone has: *"For everyone has sinned; we all fall short of God's glorious standard"* (Romans 3:23). The best and most freeing thing anyone can do is to actually give up. It is when we come to this point where we totally stop our own striving that we have a chance to experience something better.

It is when we stop our own attempts, our works, and our ideas that we can come to a place where we just say, "Jesus, you do it." Even though the Bible does not teach that we keep ourselves saved in our own strength, many have fallen in this trap. Salvation is a complete work, bought by the blood and grace of Jesus. It is a gift of God. He is, indeed, mighty to save.

Many churches have used fear-based Christianity to keep people in line, which has only added fuel to the failure mentality. It is incredible how people have made salvation seem so weak. One minute you are going to heaven, the next you are going to hell. Just say a prayer and you are going to heaven again. The work of Christ is not that cheap.

## Finally Free

The gospel is Good News because God is doing what we never could do. It is Good News not just to those perishing, but also to those who are now in our churches. Instead of living in failure, take what God is offering. Be free. It is Good News to those who thought the only way out of the battle was to run away and try to forget about it. Now, instead of running, they can rest in Jesus.

Experiencing this freedom is the beginning of a life in Christ that is actually enjoyable. When we are in Christ, all condemnation is gone. Worrying about whether or not you are good enough, clean enough, or strong enough is all history. That battle has been fought and Christ won it for us. In Him, we are clean. We are forgiven. We are free. God is actually that good.

## Advice

**FOR EVERYONE.** There is a staggering amount of people in this generation battling this one issue. We need to continue teaching the truth of the Word. It includes the message of God's mercy and grace. Go out of your way to make sure people are not falling into this trap. Teach on it. Repeat it. Repeat it again.

# It Ain't All Roses

07

# It Ain't All Roses

# 07

I love to eat. I enjoy a good meal and I love going out to res-taurants. For five years of my life, I lived in a neighbourhood on a major intersection in the suburbs of Toronto. It would not be an exaggeration to say that within five minutes of my house there was well over fifty eating establishments to choose from. I, of course, had my favourites and never made it to them all, despite my best attempts. Each one was known for certain kinds of food, certain ethnicities, or just unique styles. When I went to one of my favourite places, I knew I would have one of the best steaks I could ever have. It was always a good experience.

There is a scripture in the Bible that says, *"Taste and see the Lord is good"* (Psalm 34:8). I believe in the Word of God and that this scripture is true. Yet despite my own thoughts and beliefs, there seem to be many who have tried and have said, "No thanks." They didn't like it, didn't want it, or have spewed it out of their mouths. How is this even possible, though, if He is truly good? I believe the cause of this, or at least a part, is that we have made up our own menu instead of using God's. What people have been given and tasted is not what we said was being served.

For those of us who are believers, we cannot comprehend how anyone would not want to be a Christian. The thought that someone can sit in our services for years, hear the gospel countless times, be taught scriptures, and even spend time in the presence of God, and yet reject it all, can be offensive to us. It may not even fit with our beliefs, theology, and even scriptures like the one just mentioned.

I believe this is where listening and discernment are most important. There are issues we may not fully understand because it is not our own experience. Hearing about why many of our own children and youth have walked away, or are thinking about it, can bring a lot of insight into the struggles of this generation. It can also shed light on some of our own shortcomings.

### Advice

LISTENING CIRCLES. Listening gives us opportunity to learn. Every church needs to hear the voice of this generation before it are gone. If you are looking to help different generations understand each other, set up opportunities to let people share their thoughts and stories. This can be done in small groups, in a larger church setting, or at a special church event. It can be done in a moderated forum, with questions and answers, or discussion panels.

I have had the opportunity to be involved with these in a few different forms, and if moderated properly they can be extremely useful. People will start thinking, discussing solutions, and want to be a part of helping. This is also a useful exercise for pastoral staffs and boards.

## The Cheapening of Christianity

They were about to make the draw. Everyone was standing in anticipation to see which number was about to be drawn out of this giant spinning barrel. The night had been full of activities, bands, speakers, testimonies, gross food games, and utter madness at this all-night church youth event. This was the grand prize giveaway, which many had spent the entire night waiting for. It is why many of them were there. They were about to give away a used car.

There is nothing wrong with prizes, by the way. I actually like to win things. So do you. I recently heard of a church that was attaching an envelope with one thousand dollars to the bottom of one of the seats in their sanctuary as a way to get people out. Yet another church was giving free gas for a month to one lucky visitor.

Perhaps some of these seem ridiculous or questionable. However, every church and ministry uses some kind of hook to get people into their buildings. Yours may just not be as creative.

No matter what hook is used to get someone to an event or service, we need to be careful that what is presented is real truth. The gospel. We cannot reduce it or cheapen it. What has happened is that people have bought into a happy gospel, a cool gospel, a prize-filled gospel, a comfort gospel, an emotional gospel, a fear gospel… all of which have elements of the truth. However, they definitely do not produce repentance or long-term results.

Some Christians are in it for the prize waiting at the end. They are waiting for heaven. They may say they are a Christian because they are fearful of going to hell. There are some who have been told, "Follow Christ and your life will be perfect. Christians don't have problems, sickness, or issues." There are people who said yes to God because they have been told He is like their spiritual Santa Claus. God exists to serve them and to give them gifts.

Each one of these may have a piece of truth in them but are not how Jesus presented himself. He said, *"The kingdom of God is near. Repent and believe the good news!"* (Mark 1:15, NIV) He told people, *"Come, follow me… and I will send you out to fish for people"* (Mark 1:17, NIV). Jesus even seemed to discourage those not really interested with statements like, *"Whoever wants to be my disciple must deny themselves and take up their cross and follow me"* (Matthew 16:24, NIV). There is nothing cheap or easy in His calling to people. Neither did He use fear tactics to coerce people into the Kingdom.

There is a huge trap in trying to be cool or hip enough to reach young people. It may be with the youth worker with some kind facial hair and cool glasses who obviously spent more time on their hair than preparing for the evening's events. It can be the incredible program and entertainment. We do all kinds of things in an attempt to be relevant. If these are what we are trying to use to keep people, they will fail. Something newer will always come around. Someone or something trendier will show up. These things can actually become barriers. Youth leaders and programs can become the center of attention. Jesus must remain the centre of attention.

Things that are cheap usually break and don't last. When we present the gospel as something it isn't, people will lose interest. The result of this is that we have people who are attenders, who call themselves Christians but have never come to repentance. They have not actually decided to follow Jesus. We may be leading them somewhere, but it is not to a life-altering encounter with Jesus Christ.

If this is what people have been presented, in time they will discover it doesn't work. They have been sold something that isn't true. They will be disappointed. They will also associate this experience with Christianity and God, their minds being blinded to the truth because they were sold a cheap or counterfeit version.

## Advice

**FOR MINISTRY LEADERS.** Always promote a relationship with Jesus—One that begins with repentance and moves them into following Christ. Do all you can to promote a personal faith which is not just based on the activities of others. Teach people to pray, study, and minister on their own. Prepare them to continue in their faith for when they leave your ministry.

Do not fall for the common trap, putting most of your resources into providing activities and entertainment. These *are* important, but they must be a part of your ministry and not the whole.

## There Will Be Trials and Sorrows

God blesses. It is His promise. It states it repeatedly in the Word. He watches over us, protects us, sustains us, and hears our prayers. These are truths. Some people have taken these truths out of context and turned them into something incredibly destructive. The culture we have grown up in has affected some people's very theology.

The gospel has been presented as a shield against harm, hardships, trials, and even death. Scriptures, however, need to be looked at as a whole. An extreme prosperity-centered gospel is a false gospel. We do not just become Christians to avoid the problems of the world or just for Jesus to make our lives better. There are many benefits to living for Jesus, but prosperity is the wrong starting point.

This is so destructive because it doesn't work. Reality will prove it to be false. Sickness, death, suffering, pain, or loss will come. However, if we were promised only blessing, health, and goodness without any problems, questions will arise. Problems were definitely not on the menu. If your relationship with God is based on how well your circumstances are, it will change. When trouble comes you will ask, "Why? Why won't God listen? Doesn't God care? Isn't He able?" There will be a group that even comes to the conclusion that it was all fake.

While this may seem like a great way to present the gospel, it is shallow and wrong. The Biblical text and examples prove otherwise. Jesus told his disciples upfront that there would be trouble:

> I have told you all this so that you may have peace in me. Here on earth you will have many trials and sorrows. But take heart, because I have overcome the world. (John 16:33)

If you study the lives of the disciples and early church leaders, you will discover that their lives were far from being free of pain and sorrow. All the disciples, except one, were killed for their faith. Many were tortured and persecuted. Paul, who wrote many of the books of the New Testament, was beaten, flogged, shipwrecked, stoned, left for dead, and eventually killed. There seemed to be a huge price to pay for being a follower of Jesus. Do I believe they were blessed? Yes. Were their lives free of trouble? Definitely not.

In Hebrews 12, we receive some great instruction on how to endure and not fall away:

> Therefore, since we are surrounded by such a huge crowd of witnesses to the life of faith, let us strip off every weight that slows us down, especially the sin that so easily trips us up. And let us run with endurance the race God has set before us. We do this by keeping our eyes on Jesus, the champion who initiates and perfects our faith. Because of the joy awaiting him, he endured the cross, disregarding its shame. Now he is seated in the place of honor beside God's throne. Think of all the hostility he endured from sinful people; then you won't become weary and give up. (Hebrews 12:1–3)

We actually become stronger, building endurance by keeping our eyes on Jesus, the one who suffered for us.

When people believe in a gospel which is about freedom from problems, they end up running from God when it comes. However, when we read scriptures like these from Hebrews, we begin to understand that Jesus becomes our hope in suffering. When we have our eyes fixed on Him, we don't give up.

This scripture starts off by talking about a huge crowd of witnesses that surrounds us. I have heard many messages about the exploits of the great men and women of God mentioned in Hebrews 11, which has been coined by many as "The Hall of Faith." These mighty men of God include Enoch, Noah, Abraham.

However, there is another group of people written about. Scripture speaks very highly of them. It says, *"They were too good for this world"* (Hebrews 11:38). Who were these amazing people? They were people who had trials and hardships of many kinds. Just listen to their stories:

> But others were tortured, refusing to turn from God in order to be set free. They placed their hope in a better life after the resurrection. Some were jeered at, and their backs were cut open with whips. Others were chained in prisons. Some died by stoning, some were sawed in half, and others were killed with the sword. Some went about wearing skins of sheep and goats, destitute and oppressed and mistreated. (Hebrews 11:35–37)

Trials, torture, chains, prisons, and even death were not signs of sin, that God had forsaken them, or that God never heard their cries. Instead, through His Word He lifts them up as examples. They are the great crowd of witnesses. We are, in fact, surrounded by those who have suffered. They are cheering us on.

We cannot reduce the gospel to a blessing-only gospel. Trouble will come, and unless there is a proper foundation, it will destroy people's faith. The stories of the men and women in the Bible must be told. The good, the difficult, and the real. We don't have to go looking for trials and hardships; they will find us sooner or later all on their own. It is through these times that we need to lean on God more, as it creates perseverance and maturity in us.

## Advice

**TESTIMONIES.** We can sometimes limit the stories we tell to the "miracle moments." We also need to hear the stories of how God brought people through sickness, abuse, the loss of a family member, jobs, or trials. These will help dispel the notion that Christians do not hurt, struggle, or face huge obstacles in life.

**RESOURCES.** There are some amazing books in print which tell the stories of average people who endured many trials and even death. An early work is *Foxe's Book of Martyrs.* [2] There are also a few modern titles, like *Jesus Freaks.*[3]

## False Success

One of the reasons we cannot accept trouble of any kind is that we have a worldly view of what success is. I have seen firsthand some of the amazing things being done by young people around the world. Whether it is planting churches, starting movements, or raising incredible amounts of money for relief and missions, young people are doing amazing things. It seems that some people, even in their youth, are able to see and believe God for great things. We should not be surprised. The Bible speaks about what will happen in the last days:

---

2    Forbush, William Byron *Foxe's Book of Martyrs* (Chicago, IL: Holt, Rinehart, and Winston, 1926).

3    DC Talk and Voice of the Martyrs. *Jesus Freaks* (Tulsa, OK: Albury Publishing, 1999).

> I will pour out my Spirit upon all people. Your sons
> and daughters will prophesy. Your old men will
> dream dreams, and your young men will see visions.
> (Joel 2:28)

I have attended more children's, youth, and young adult events, camps, retreats, and conventions than I can count. A common theme among them is believing for God to do great things in their day. Another theme is that young people need to have God-sized dreams and visions. I certainly pray that God actually does even greater things in this generation than I even have faith for.

As leaders and parents, we need to portray what real success is. We can be guilty of presenting something that may be "church" success, but not Godly success. The dreams and visions God gives will always bring glory to Him. The visions God gave many of those in the Bible often led to great victories, some to persecution, some to great sacrifice, and some to death.

In the book of John, we see Jesus teaching a lesson which He had already repeated several times. I believe this lesson was repeated again and again because it was one of the disciples' biggest struggles. It is also one of the modern church's entanglements. It is about success and greatness, and what it really is. It is here at the last supper that one of the strongest rebukes in all of Scripture is recorded.

> Before the Passover celebration, Jesus knew that his
> hour had come to leave this world and return to his
> Father. He had loved his disciples during his min-
> istry on earth, and now he loved them to the very

> end. It was time for supper, and the devil had already prompted Judas, son of Simon Iscariot, to betray Jesus. Jesus knew that the Father had given him authority over everything and that he had come from God and would return to God. So he got up from the table, took off his robe, wrapped a towel around his waist, and poured water into a basin. Then he began to wash the disciples' feet, drying them with the towel he had around him.
>
> When Jesus came to Simon Peter, Peter said to him, "Lord, are you going to wash my feet?"
>
> Jesus replied, "You don't understand now what I am doing, but someday you will."
>
> "No," Peter protested, "you will never ever wash my feet!"
>
> Jesus replied, "Unless I wash you, you won't belong to me."
>
> Simon Peter exclaimed, "Then wash my hands and head as well, Lord, not just my feet!" (John 13:1–9)

Later during the evening, Jesus also tells Peter that he is going to deny Him three times before morning. At that point, Jesus doesn't give Peter the severe rebuke He receives here. He is basically telling Peter, "If you don't let me do this, go home. We're done." I have heard it argued that the foot-washing is a sign of our need to be cleansed if we are to belong to Christ. That may be true, but we may be missing the obvious.

I believe this strong rebuke took place because of what happened prior to Jesus washing the disciples' feet. It is one of several accounts where the disciples broke out in an argument about which of them would be the greatest.

> Then they began to argue among themselves about who would be the greatest among them.
>
> Jesus told them, "In this world the kings and great men lord it over their people, yet they are called 'friends of the people.' But among you it will be different. Those who are the greatest among you should take the lowest rank, and the leader should be like a servant. Who is more important, the one who sits at the table or the one who serves? The one who sits at the table, of course. But not here! For I am among you as one who serves." (Luke 22:24–27)

Here, Jesus gives some clear direction on how His Kingdom works. It is not the same as the world. What is great elsewhere is not great here. Jesus even acknowledges how things work in the world, but *"among you it will be different."* Those who are disciples of Christ have to have a different idea of what greatness is. The greatest must be the least. In verse 27, after explaining how things in the kingdom of the world work, He says, *"But not here."* There is no room for self-glory, self-promotion, or worldly thinking. This is the Upside-Down Kingdom.

Peter was in no way being disrespectful when he said Jesus could not wash his feet. In his upbringing, he learned to respect those in leadership, and here was the Messiah attempting to take the role of a servant. He was acting according to what was normal, the way the world works. But again, listen to the words of Jesus. "But not here. With you it will be different."

Our actions as leaders and parents show what we believe success is. For example, parents will invest tens of thousands of dollars on their children's education but never consider investing a portion of that amount in the spiritual upbringing of their kids. When we send our kids off to university, we make sure they have their courses picked, their books bought, and a place to live. Do we find a faith community for them to connect to?

When I heat speakers talking about having God-sized dreams, they're often talking about speaking in front of thousands of people, leading a worship team, or leading some kind of ministry. While I hope many end up in those positions, the truth is, if we want to be great we have to desire to serve. A God-sized dream may even cause you to disappear.

True success in this life is living like Jesus. It involves carrying a cross. It may take us around the world sharing the gospel. It may take us to the extremely needy ends of the earth. It may take us to the drug addict living under a bridge in our own community. That is success. We need to make sure we never think we are too good to do what Jesus did.

## Does It Work?

Remember when I told you about the shadow miracle, when Peter healed a man with his shadow? While you may not have tried this before, I would test it out. You will need to wait until there is a sunny day, or perhaps purchase a really bright light. Then, when the conditions are right, go find someone who has some physical problem. Walk past them and see if they are healed when your shadow passes over them. While it is true that the Apostle Peter's shadow ministry worked quite well, mine sure doesn't.

As you are reading this book, a broken shadow ministry may or may not be an issue for you. There is such variation in what churches teach and believe on the miraculous or how God works today. However, this has implications for us all.

One of the common terms associated with Christians is the word hypocrite. I think there are lots of bad examples of hypocrites over the years which has led to that association. When we think of that word, we may only associate it with sin—someone who says they are one thing but living another. However, as a church we can say we are something but be something entirely different.

We can say we are loving, and not be. We can say we are accepting, and not be. We can say we work in the power of the Holy Spirit and miracles happen, but no one ever sees it. We can say God heals, and that it is His will, but no miracles happen. This has been the story of many youth and young adults I have interviewed. Even a close friend told me, "In all my days of attending church, I never saw anything that convinced me it was real." This had to do with his perception that if the supernatural wasn't seen, then God must not be present or real.

We certainly need to believe in the greatness of God, the unexpected, and the impossible. The Bible is full of examples of incredible faith, stories of how God broke into the normal everyday lives of people and the supernatural took place. These miracles range from healing to the dead being raised, from nations being saved from disaster to God providing food. These are all part of the story of the church.

Here, though, lies the struggle for many. When they are taught something but don't see it, questions and doubt arise. When a friend or family faces sickness, what will happen? What happens when their prayers don't seem to get answered? Over and over again, I have watched people stricken with tragedy or sickness run to God. There are also those who run the other way. People have questioned, *Did I not have enough faith? Does God not care for me as much as the people that God did heal? Maybe God can't do anything. Maybe the Bible is wrong. Maybe my church is wrong. Maybe He isn't real at all.*

The answer cannot be to lower our standards. Instead, we simply need to be what we say we are. I do believe in miracles. However, I have never walked on water. That does not mean I don't believe Jesus did. I know God heals. I also know people who died after being prayed for.

As stated at the beginning of the chapter, if we put something on the menu, but it is never served, it leads to disillusionment. Some people have claimed that their church has written a cheque they can never cash. What if some of the things we tell everyone will happen, never happen? What if our promises turn up empty?

This is one topic which I personally struggle with—trying to find the balance between the reality of living in a broken world and knowing the Kingdom of God is at hand. I am not even sure if we are supposed to have a balance. I have my own questions for God as to why I have friends who have experienced miracles while other friends succumb to sickness.

I have concluded that I must live in expectation. I want to live a life of awe. Perhaps God is so big, so great, so mysterious that I won't understand it all this side of heaven. I certainly want, and try, to live a life of faith. I want to live in a way that pleases God, living like Jesus the best I can—in speech, action, character, and even in the power of the Holy Spirit.

I realize that our faith comes from more than just our teaching to people. The Apostle Paul writes:

> For when we brought you the Good News, it was not only with words but also with power, for the Holy Spirit gave you full assurance[ that what we said was true. And you know of our concern for you from the way we lived when we were with you. (1 Thessalonians 1:5)

We cannot diminish the word of the Holy Spirit.

I am so thankful that God does work today. When I have seen things happen which are simply unexpected and impossible, I am reminded of the greatest of the God we serve. I hope everyone has these experiences which remind them how real God is.

I have also concluded that miracles or repeated signs of the supernatural will not keep people in their churches. While I know many would disagree, I want to point out a few Biblical examples. The Israelites, who had a pillar of fire and a cloud of smoke hovering over them, questioned, doubted, and rebelled against Moses and God. They were brought out of Egypt and all would have personally witnessed the plagues and the power of God. Another example is Jesus. Thousands saw Him perform miraculous signs and wonders. Even Judas would have witnessed Jesus bringing people back from the dead. However, all the witnesses of these events did not follow Him. "shock and awe," on its own, does not retain.

However, a faith without *faith* is nothing. It is dead, useless, and doesn't help retain anyone. In the end, we need to seek after God. We can agree with the prophet Habakkuk, who said, *"Lord, I have heard of your fame; I stand in awe of your deeds, Lord. Repeat them in our day, in our time make them known; in wrath remember mercy"* (Habakkuk 3:2, NIV). We are even instructed to eagerly desire spiritual gifts. We need to be faithful to the Word of God.

Trouble, sickness, and loss will come to us all. Life isn't all roses, but through it all we are promised we have *"a friend who sticks closer than a brother"* (Proverbs 18:24, NIV). In our troubles, we can go to the one who also suffered. We can run to the one who overcame.

We can believe for God to work in the big things in life. We also can see God in everyday lives. He sustains us. Every perfect gift comes from Him. Truthfully, the miraculous is always happening. Our eyes are blinded to it because we have narrow sight. The fact that our world exists is a testimony to a creative miracle. That fact that matter stays together is unexplainable. Your body is a living miracle in the complexity of creation. The fact that we can love defies explanation. God is, indeed, at work.

## Advice

**FOR EVERYONE.** We need to teach on how God is ever-present and ever-working. We need to make sure people understand that if they don't "feel" something, it doesn't mean it is gone. We need to make sure it is understood that our lives are made up of many types of experiences. There are moments when we feel close to God, and other moments when God seems so far away.

When trouble comes, it is actually okay to admit that we don't know why everything happens.

# Be Careful Little Eyes

# Be Careful Little Eyes

# 08

There is no possible way to adequately deal with all the topics which will be mentioned here in one chapter, or even one book. There are certainly differing opinions on a few of the following topics, even in Christian circles. No matter what each of our opinions may be, I am very certain that many in this generation are asking questions about the issues about to be mentioned. My hope is that the following words will help start a conversation and point you to resources to help answer a few of the questions people are asking.

## The Bible

Many people, while they may be struggling with church attendance, are certainly not turning their backs on God. At the same time, there is also what appears to be a growing number of people who say they are rejecting religion, and specifically Christianity. At the core of their arguments is, in fact, the Bible.

> **"**
> Cover to cover reading is enough to sour any thoughtful person on the vindictive, chariot-riding, volcano god of the Hebrew scriptures.
> **"**

Just broaching this subject in various settings as I travel brings up much emotion. To even mention it seems to be quite offensive, as we certainly hold the Bible in highest regard. It truly is the Word of God, the truth, and it is God-breathed. It is God's revealed message to us. Millions, if not billions, after hearing the truth found in Scripture have been saved. If this is all true, how could it even be possible for someone to say they are rejecting the Christian faith because of it?

As I have researched the kinds of messages and material found on the internet about Christianity, I have found a lot of negativity. Most of the material is aimed at discrediting our faith and giving reasons to avoid it, reject it, and oppose it. The most common denominator in all of this material is, indeed, the Bible.

This is not a new issue. There have always been people who argued against the existence of God, Christianity, the Bible, and faith in general. However, things have changed. The sheer volume of material has exploded as quickly as the internet has grown. The age at which this material is aimed is changing. At one time, these challenges were things our students dealt with primarily in university, but today it is hitting kids and youth of all ages.

This, coupled with the fact that it is no longer taboo to publicly criticize, demean, or disagree with the Bible, has created a new world. In society, respect for the church, those who lead it, and the Bible has certainly declined. The attack on the Bible is now an acceptable practice.

You should be aware, whether you are a pastor, leader, or parent, that most of the material available to this generation questions the credibility of everything you teach. This is an attack against the actual foundations of our faith. Against the reliability of scripture, the deity of Christ. These arguments question whether or not Christianity is a religion of hate and intolerance. Without a strong foundation, a house falls.

We would like to believe that this movement is only being spearheaded by bitter, disillusioned, or uninformed former churchgoers. Perhaps there are some of those involved, but this movement is also being championed by intelligent, well-spoken, sincere, and even well-intentioned men and women. Many, to their knowledge, are doing this in a sincere attempt to make the world a better place for themselves and future generations. For example, they would believe that by removing religion they can stop the needless discrimination, abuse, war, and death of millions, which happens all the time in the name of god.

## Can I Just Ask You One Question?

I have been involved in countless outreach events around the world, and have seen and heard of many others. One of the common approaches to sharing the gospel with people has been to start by asking a question. "Do you believe you are good person?" or "Have you ever done anything wrong?" are some starting points aimed at getting people to recognize their need of a saviour. Why do Christian ministries and groups use these approaches? Because they help to start a conversation about faith, and to introduce Jesus.

Today this same approach is being used to try to convince our youth that they should leave their faith behind. They are being asked how they can serve a God who promotes things as repulsive as slavery. *"However, you may purchase male and female slaves from among the nations around you"* (Leviticus 25:44). Or, if God is truly a loving God, why did He command the killing of children? *"But the Lord our God handed him over to us, and we crushed him, his sons, and all his people. We conquered all his towns and completely destroyed everyone—men, women, and children. Not a single person was spared"* (Deuteronomy 2:33–34).

> **"**
>
> As I read the Bible, it just didn't make sense. I didn't want to justify atrocious acts in the Old Testament anymore. I didn't understand all the contradictions. I didn't see how God could be so loving and yet such a jerk at the same time. So I started researching both apologetic websites and atheist websites to see what they had to say. And I thought that the atheist arguments made way more sense.
>
> **"**

We live in a day and age where intolerance is not accepted and those who commit atrocities are criminals. Does a young person know how to answer why the angel of the Lord was responsible for the death of the firstborn of every family in Egypt? (Exodus 12:29) Why God Himself sent wild beasts to kill children? (Leviticus 26:22) How could God command or even allow such a perversion where a society was massacred but the Israelite men got to take all the young girls for themselves? *"So kill all the boys and all the women who have had intercourse with a man. Only the young girls who are virgins may live; you may keep them for yourselves"* (Numbers 31:17–18).

Hundreds of examples from the Bible are being used to convince this generation that the Bible is not a message of hope and love. Instead it promotes hate, intolerance, injustice, discrimination, and extremism. In fact, the same arguments Christians have used against other religions—such as Islam and the Koran—are being used against us.

With the opening of the information highway, the difficult, mis-understood, and just hard to understand issues in the Bible are on display for all to see. So is everyone's opinion on each of them. Many of these arguments and scriptures may be taken out of context, out of their cultural relevance or time period. However, no matter where or how they are coming up, they are being used to present the Bible and Christianity as absolute lunacy in our society today.

What I have found incredibly sad is the large number of young adults who have been affected by this. I have been told how many went looking for answers, but received none, even in the church. They have been told not to question, just to accept. "It was just culture," they were told dismissively. To them, it seemed that those asking the questions seemed to know more, so perhaps they were right.

I have also discovered something else. The reason most youth leaders, church leaders, parents, and ministers don't have a re-sponse is because they either have the same questions, or they do not know the answers themselves. It appears to most of this new, struggling generation that the church has had no response, which adds to the doubt that has already planted.

## The Intolerance of the Religious

It has been claimed that there are more people facing persecution, discrimination, mistreatment, imprisonment, and death for their faith today than at any other time in history. Along with the arguments about the Bible and our own past, the attacks against religion and Christianity are based on current events. The evils being done in the name of God today are all the proof many need to conclude that the world would be better off without God.

The attacks against our faith, of course, come from many sources. The devil is trying to destroy lives. Many arguments and lies come right from him. There are many who are acting out of hurt and bitterness, who want revenge against the church because of things that have been done to them personally. There are also those who are trying to rid the world of religion in order to make it a better place.

This last group of people would argue that religion is the fuel that sparks extremism. That religion has the ability to manipulate and control people. That the evils of war, hatred, genocide, terrorism, and various atrocities are happening because of religion. The Bible and other religious books have been used to say we have been doing this for thousands of years. Our own story of crusades show that they continued in more recent history, and today it seems no better. The reason so many of our own are believing the message that the world may be a better place without religion is that, in part, it may be true.

It is a fact that evil has been done, and is being done, in the name of God. It is true that many of the earth's conflicts have revolved around religious beliefs. Today, as you are reading these words, people are being killed, abused, raped, mistreated, and persecuted in the name of religion and some god. It is undeniable that Christians have been part of this throughout history. We even have modern day examples of Catholics and Protestants at war, killing each other.

> **"** In college, we were taught not what to think, but how to think. As I read the Bible and tried my best to put aside contrived interpretations that I had been taught, I gradually found that the story as I read it was vastly different from the things being taught in the church. **"**

Would the world be better without all of this pain and suffering? Yes, it would. I actually agree with much of what many of the modern day sceptics are saying. I do, however, disagree with their conclusions. I agree that the world would be better off without religion that causes the horrific things mentioned above. However, the world needs to see the kind of religion, mentioned in James, which takes care of the widows and orphans and keeps us pure. The world does not want a religion which creates the spark of incredible suffering. The world does need a God who gives hope to the hopeless, who loves, and who saves.

> But in your hearts revere Christ as Lord. Always be
> prepared to give an answer to everyone who asks you
> to give the reason for the hope that you have. But do
> this with gentleness and respect, keeping a clear con-
> science, so that those who speak maliciously against
> your good behavior in Christ may be ashamed of their
> slander. (1 Peter 3:15–16, NIV)

We are not the first generation who has had our faith questioned.
Just imagine for a moment the adversity and challenges the early
church faced. They were introducing people to Jesus, who many
had never even heard of. They also faced challenges from those
who did not recognize Jesus as the Messiah. Added to that there
would have been many who wondered how He could be the one
true God in the midst of the thousands of gods they already had.
Much of the New Testament records the struggles of presenting
the gospel. People were rejected, scoffed, thrown in prison, beaten,
and killed. Today we seemed shocked when people write books
against our faith.

### Advice

**BE PREPARED.** In the middle of that kind of challenge, the Apostle
Peter gives us several pieces of advice in how to deal with this.
First, we need to be prepared to give an answer for what we believe. When it comes to defending the Bible, most of our youth
have not been given the tools they need to deal with the questions
people are raising. They are not prepared, and many didn't even
know the questions existed, which has left them blindsided.

There is no shortcut to learning. It takes listening, studying, reading, and work. If we are to be able to give an answer from the Bible, we need people who know what is in it. There is a need for churches and generational ministries to talk and discuss even the difficult issues.

The Apostle Peter also advises that we are to do this with gentleness and respect. This is where many churches struggle. When questioned, they lash out, mock, and use the "How can you question God?" approach, thereby push it under the carpet. However, it is not just those outside the church who have these questions; it is those inside. Our attitudes often convince people who have no idea what we are talking about.

> "
> No one in the church wanted to talk about the issues that bothered me and I quickly learned they did not have a clue about their theology. What was worse was that professors, pastors, and colleagues all knew the issues but refused to talk about them in public for fear that it would agitate their positions.
> "

**TELL THE TRUTH.** In this chapter, I gave a few examples of stories people use to question the Bible. If you do a quick search on the internet, you will discover that there are literally hundreds of others. No person can say that there are not difficult issues in the

Bible. Too often, when confronted with difficult issues in the Bible, we shout back about its infallibility. However, we are not as quick to explain what the implications of that belief are.

In no way does admitting that there are hard or difficult issues in the Bible negate its truth. Jesus Himself kept up His teaching, and people would leave. At one point He asked His disciples if they were leaving, too. There are stories in Bible that are not always easy to understand. If it was, we would not have tens of thousands of different Christian denominations and sects all believing that they have it right.

I believe it it better that this generation hears about questions being raised from you than those trying to destroy their faith. Encourage people to ask about the questions they have. You can even bring them up. It is actually more helpful to admit that you don't have all the answers. These are times when together you can make discoveries, search out truth, and find answers.

**PROVIDING RESOURCES.** I was blessed to sit under the teaching of Dr. Scott Bullerwell, who is an Old Testament scholar. Some of the issues mentioned were discussed in my classes with him. However, the vast majority of Christians never have that opportunity, but the material is indeed available. Many churches struggle with answers, so having resources and knowing where to point people is very important.

We have been blessed with many great writers and gifted apologetics. There are many great resources, materials, websites, and individuals to turn to if you are dealing with these questions. At the end of this chapter, there is a list of a few books, websites, and ministries which can be of great help. However, if you do a few quick searches online, you will discover just how much good material is actually available.

**SPEAK TRUTH.** While sceptics and attackers may say differently, there are in fact many good explanations to many of these issues being raised. Much of the negative information being presented comes from false assumptions, lies mixed with truth, scriptures being used out of context, and all of this coming from people who do not know the full history or culture of the times in which the Bible was written. Our youth need to know that much of these arguments actually come from people without belief in God, in sin and its consequences, and people who may be blind to the truth.

**LIVING IT.** Lastly, Saint Peter really answers how we are meant to handle ourselves personally in this day. We need to make sure our lives exemplify Christ's likeness. Our present good deeds and actions need to outweigh the sins of the past. Basically, it is time that people felt uncomfortable putting the church and Christians down because of the good they do.

We need to tell the story of how societies are better places because of the Bible and Christianity. The entire planet owes so much to men and women of God who spearheaded the end of slavery, who brought us health care, social justice, court systems, humanitarian organizations, and educational systems. The work of Christ in the lives of regular people has brought real and positive changes to society as a whole.

There is also the testimony of millions and millions of people who have been transformed by the Word of God. Our young people need to be aware that the testimonies of those who have been saved are just as valid as those who say otherwise. It starts with letting others see how your life has been transformed by the Word of God. Show this generation how you, living by the words of Jesus, are making a difference in this life.

> "
> I personally never found an argument for Christianity that was compelling in the first place. There were too many loopholes—conflicting scriptures, picking and choosing what to believe from the Bible and what not to, etc. Am I only believing this because I was born in a certain part of the world?
> "

### Advice

Mark Griffin, an international speaker and life coach, writes:

I don't wanna sound like a broken record here, but I've noticed David Sawler talks a lot about genuine and authentic relationship in his writing and speaking. One huge component of this authenticity is listening... and I know you've heard it from him before, but when are we actually going to embrace this fundamental characteristic of Jesus' lifestyle in our narcissistic and preachy little church world?

I met a guy an on airplane a few years back. We were both heading west on a laboriously slow milk run of a flight that stopped in most Canadian cities west of Ottawa. Suffice to say, we had a lot of time to chat. Over the course of the first hour, I found out he was raised as a young man in a great evangelical church. He clearly knew the gospel and yet had chosen to become a part of the goodbye generation; not presently interested in church one little bit.

Over the next few hours, I listened to his heart. He *had* been interested in the faith, profoundly so. His issue was that he had some concerns over a fundamental doctrine question—how do we know the Bible is the actual word of God and not just a collection of stories? He asked his youth leader, his Sunday school teacher, and his pastor; he essentially got the same response on every level. "It just is! Why can't you just accept it?"

This young man (now in his thirties) didn't have the benefit of a search engine to find his answers by himself back in the early 90s, and so he consequently lost his way with the faith. But the thing that stuck with me is that he said he had heard plenty of sermons, so he knew a *lot* of the word. But he said, "Everyone in church was answering questions that no one was asking."

I just wanna be the first to say, as a youth worker and church leader for two and a half decades... I've crapped the bed on that one. As a parent, too. Genuine listening puts people in a safe place where they can get *their* questions answered and develop a real faith of their own. I wanna be that kind of leader, parent, and friend to this generation.

– Mark Griffin, Germany

www.markgriffin.ca

## The Intolerance of the Church

In an earlier chapter, we discussed how people have found some churches less than loving and accepting. Again, as long as there are imperfect people in churches, there will be failings. It is true that throughout history the church has had people who have made both good and bad decisions. However, one particular piece of ammunition being used against us, to show how intolerant we really are, are the actions we take against each other.

One question which seems to come up in both the Christian and non-Christian settings is this: if we are truly a religion based on the love of God, why is the church so fragmented? The church is divided into tens of thousands of different denominations, sects, and organizations around the world. If Jesus' prayer and desire was that we were to be "one," then it would appear we have missed the goal.

We may be able to say we no longer kill those who don't agree with us, or burn people at the stake, but we are being questioned about some of our present actions. For a group that talks about love, grace, acceptance, and the family of God, it may appear we can only walk the walk with those who completely agree with us.

When we examine the material on the internet, which is from so-called "Christian" sources, this issue become quite obvious. It seems every church leader, ministry, and denomination has many people who are involved with them, and also a huge group of people who take significant time to let the rest of the world know what is wrong with them. Our arguments against each other are out in the open for all to see. The actions of Christians have caused people to say, "If that is what Christians are like, let's stay away."

There is a trend that has become the norm today. It is rare for someone to join a church because of its denomination. This may have been true of early generations, but it's certainly not true of this one. As our society has become more tolerant of religions, beliefs, and different opinions, many have been left wondering why the church is so behind. This trend may not be a totally correct one, as theology is important. However, what we are seeing is that people are choosing acceptance, family, and proximity over differing opinions. I struggle with this issue as a minister because I hope that the values and perspectives on scripture are being picked up by those we teach.

Through hearing people's stories and doing research, I have come to a conclusion: churches that disregard the larger body of Christ, or who set their priorities on pointing out the faults of other believers, do damage to themselves and those in their churches. It appears that the groups who have tried to pull inward, protect, and shelter their young from the "evils" in the rest of the body (which they likely do not believe are actually part of the body), are the ones who lose the most in the end. If you are the only one who thinks you are right, it may be true, but there is the real possibility that you are wrong.

There is an incredible need for proper theology. The scriptures clearly teach that He has set some people apart to be teachers, those who will be used to guide us. I am part of a denomination and am under a covering. I personally think that everyone should be part of some kind of accountability structure. How then should we treat those who differ in opinion on some matters of faith and belief? In the end, we all may have feelings or opinions about this. However, we do need to ask what the results of our actions are in the lives of those we are leading. In this topic, I can only offer my own opinion, which may be far from perfect.

### Beautiful Diversity

There is, in fact, beauty in diversity. We are not all the same. There are people who will connect to God through music. Some will be drawn to very intellectual discussions about God. Some people are very emotional and need to connect on a heart level. Perhaps just as in creation, God made each of us different so that we would need different groups for different types of people. This is not a bad thing at all. In fact, it's what makes us a body. We are not all just an "eye" or a "hand." As long as each part can still recognize that the other is still a part of the same body, it can be healthy.

We can sometimes view denominations as evil, political, or controlling, but they can in fact be of great benefit. They have been a source of collective mission, because as a group we can send people and conduct projects which would be impossible in a smaller setting. Denominations can bring accountability and a Godly covering to those who work within it. They are also a great connecting point to other churches and the greater family of God.

The reason why some have focused on the division is because differences have been handled the wrong way. If you have a problem with a brother, the Bible first instructs that we are to go to them. What we are seeing is that people have made these open issues for the world to see. Correction does not need to be done in public, except perhaps in extreme circumstances.

In dealing with this generation, our goal must be to keep this generation's eyes fixed on Jesus. My desire is that children, young people, and adults know and experience Christ in His fullness. We must make sure that this is our goal first and foremost, and not just to make them part of any particular denomination. In the end, I would be happy to see my children attending any Bible-believing church than not attending any church at all.

## Advice

**FOR EVERYONE.** Celebrate your distinctiveness as a church and denomination. Also, celebrate the body of Christ. It is a healthy exercise to join together in corporate settings for worship and teaching. We should also join in mission with people of other denominations and church structures. Coming together in this way opens people's eyes to the large body of Christ and how God truly is at work all around the world.

## The Hidden Reason Why Kids Leave the Faith

Sean McDowell, who is a speaker, teacher, and apologist, suggests that there may be even more factors accounting for why youth struggle with faith and beliefs. He writes:

> There has been much talk recently about why kids leave the faith after high school graduation. Research shows that the lack of training in apologetics and worldviews is one of the prime reasons. Kids simply don't have good reasons for their beliefs and are often crushed by professors who subtly or overtly challenge their faith.

> But there is another, perhaps more important, reason kids leave the faith. It's the elephant in the room. And I'm amazed how few people talk about it. The reason is psychological. Psychologist Paul Vitz is well known for his book *The Faith of the Fatherless*, in which he shows how the great atheists of the past

almost universally had distant, dead, or harsh fathers. He calls this "the theory of the defective father." According to Vitz, once a child is disappointed in or loses respect for his or her earthly father, then belief in a heavenly father become virtually impossible.

Vitz supports his case by pointing to the lives of prominent atheists such as Sigmund Freud, Jean-Paul Sartre, Karl Marx, Bertrand Russell, Madalyn Murray O'Hair, Friedrich Nietzsche, and many more. Freud, for example, had a father who was passive, weak, a sexual pervert, and unable to provide financially for his family. Vitz says, "One other thing, his father was closely associated with religion, especially Judaism, because as Freud got older his father began to read a good deal of Jewish Scripture and things like that. So for Freud his father stood for religion, specifically for Judaism, and he also stood for weakness, incompetence and perhaps perversion."[4] Clearly, there were many reasons Freud wanted to distance himself from his disappointing father.

Vitz does not present these examples as arguments for theism as that would commit the genetic fallacy. But he aims to show how powerfully psychological factors, and especially the relationship with the father, influence our beliefs, whether conscious or unconscious. In fact, he believes the major barriers to belief in God are not rational but psychological. Psychological factors

---

4    Vitz, Paul. "The Psychology of Atheism," in A Place for Truth, edited by Dallas Willard (Downers Grove, IL: InterVarsity Press, 2010), p. 146.

are not determinative, but strongly shape our perception and approach to God whether we realize it or not.

To see how this relates to kids leaving the faith, let's briefly consider Vitz's own story. He grew up in a "wishy-washy" Christian home in the Midwest. He became an atheist in grad school and remained so until his re-conversion back to Christianity in his late thirties. While he would have denied it at the time, he now realizes that his reasons for becoming an atheist from eighteen to thirty-eight were "intellectually superficial and largely without a deep thought basis."[5] Vitz is convinced that this phenomenon is widespread today.

Rather than reasoning to his atheistic beliefs, he was simply socialized into them. He cites three reasons for his initial conversion. First, he had a degree of social unease coming from the Midwest. It seemed terribly dull, provincial, middle class, and narrow. He wanted to be part of the glamorous secular world at Michigan when he arrived on campus as an undergrad. Just think about all the young people arriving in New York, Los Angeles, Chicago or other big cities or campuses who are embarrassed by their fundamental upbringing. This kind of socialization, says Vitz, has pushed many people away from God.

Second, he wanted to be accepted by the powerful and influential people in his field of psychology. His professors at Stanford had two things in common—

5    Ibid., p. 138.

their intense ambition and rejection of religion. Vitz concludes, "In this environment, just as I had learned how to dress like a college student by putting on the right clothes, I also learned to think like a proper psychologist by putting on the right, that is, atheistic or skeptical, ideas and attitudes."[6]

The third factor is personal convenience. Vitz explains, "The fact is, it is quite inconvenient to be a serious believer in today's neo-pagan world. I would have to give up many pleasures, some money and a good deal of time. I didn't have enough pleasures, I didn't have enough time, and I didn't have enough money to do any of that as far as I was concerned."[7] Doubts about God often follow when young people grasp how inconvenient Christianity can really be. I've had countless discussions with young people about God, the Bible, evolution, and other apologetic issues only to discover that what is really driving their doubts is immoral behavior (usually sex). This is not always true, but I'm surprised how many times it is.

Combine all these factors and we can see why many kids leave the faith. When young people go off to college there is no accountability structure and the separation from family often creates an even deeper desire to fit in with the crowd. Given that we are like sheep, as Jesus so memorably put it, there's no wonder so many kids abandon their faith in the midst of social pressure.

6   Ibid., p. 139.

7   Ibid., pp. 139–140.

The purpose of this article is not to downplay the role of apologetics in preparing our kids for life. I firmly believe it is one of the biggest pieces still largely missing from children's and youth ministry. But we must also address the psychological and social reasons that shape belief and unbelief. If we don't, it may not matter how persuasive our apologetics are.

– Sean McDowell

www.seanmcdowell.org

# Things Change

09

# Things Change

# 09

Things change. Sometimes things change so fast that it puts everything and everyone into unknown territory. We are certainly living in one of those times right now. No generation has ever had the visual, audio, media, and information stimulation that young people have today.

There are young people who do not know of a world without computers, texting, Facebook, the internet, and instant access to everything. Sexting, which wasn't even a word a few years ago, is a normal part of many teens' lives. Pornography is now considered part of the culture. It is available to children and youth on every computer and handheld device. What was taboo is now totally and instantly accessible.

While many people can speculate, no one knows for sure what the outcome of all this will be. People's lives are lived in the open. Every good and ugly thing you do in public will be in pics, blogs, and video for the rest of your lives. Mistakes will not be forgotten. Besides the ramifications all of this is having on our personal lives, it is also affecting the faith of our young people.

## The New Reality

There is one shift that leaders and ministers must recognize as we walk into this new territory: the internet has changed everything. It is already affecting us more than we realize.

For the past two thousand years, the main source of information about Jesus and Christianity was passed on through the spoken word. The invention of the printing press brought on a revolution where the Bible was put into the hands of normal people. It spawned a new era that helped spread the gospel and change the face of Christianity around the world.

We have now entered into the next revolution. The main source of information, for almost everything, is now the internet. It is the place people go to learn about Jesus, religion, and Christianity. The new reality is that the church is not the main source of information anymore about religion and Christianity. The outcome of this new reality is uncertain, but we are already seeing a few trends.

## In Search of Answers

I was sitting in a youth service being held for mostly unchurched youth. The leaders were leading a question and answer time about many of the questions the students had about faith and Christianity. Discussion was going on in every subject area from the crusades to how Jesus is different than other religious leaders. These youth were actually searching and wrestling with what they were hearing.

At the end of the discussion, the leader told the kids they would continue the discussion the following week. She also gave them an assignment. She told them to do some research and read about some of the issues they had talked about that evening. Then, the next week, they would further discuss what they had found out.

This seems like a great idea. It is when people discover and encounter the truth that they are set free. So why not help them find it? There is, however, a problem with this advice. Where were these youth going to go in search of answers? Perhaps, as many as one hundred percent of them would go to the internet.

So I tried an experiment. I would encourage you to test this yourself to see the results. I did some searches on YouTube and Google on some of the things discussed. On average, only a small percentage of the information, sites, and videos would contain anything that this leader wanted these youth to find. Instead there were endless articles, videos, and sites dedicated to why Christianity is not right, why it is evil, why no person in their right mind would listen to Christians.

For example, if you type in the word "Bible" or "is the Bible true" on YouTube or Google, you will find that most of the material found is discussing why the Bible is *not* true. There will be many sites asking how it is even possible that any reasonable person can serve a God who does the things mentioned in the Old Testament. The list goes on and on. It is actually shocking to find out many individuals, groups, and organizations have dedicated themselves to destroying faith in God, and specifically in Jesus and the church.

This generation is living in a time where their number one source of information is declaring that their faith is false, can't be trusted, and may even be evil. In church, they may hear how Jesus is the only one who ever rose again, but they will hear and read on the internet that many religions have made the same claims of their God. They will hear in church how we are to love our enemies, but will read about how the church ordered and promoted the crusades. They can hear about acceptance and forgiveness on a Sunday, but in their room read about how Christians burned people at the stake. This has led to the church's claims being called into question. It is an attack on the very foundations of faith, in the deity of Jesus, and the credibility of the Word of God.

## Picturing the Net

If you want a true picture of what is on the internet when it comes to Christianity, go to a regular bookstore. Go to the Christianity or Religion section. I am disappointed every time I have done this myself. The vast majority of texts, even as much as ninety percent, are not pro-Christian. Very often, the most popular and bestselling books in the Christian section are there to discredit Christianity.

This picture is a pretty accurate representation of what is on the internet about Christianity. It saddens me to think that if someone came into one of these stores honestly seeking God, they would not be led to the truth. If a young person does any search about Jesus, Christianity, or related topics, they are more likely to get something aimed at discrediting their faith than to find something helpful. While it's true that the internet has so much good material, we have to be aware of what else is on it. We have to understand that there are now endless people and organizations who have made it their mission to save this generation from your church and from faith in God. They are creative, convincing and deceiving many.

### Advice

**POINT PEOPLE IN THE RIGHT DIRECTION.** When I want to look up a particular verse in the Bible, I use a familiar site called Bible Gateway. It is a simple site which has a few Bible versions readily available. I don't have to fight through endless garbage to find it, because I know where it is and that the information there is reliable.

Be proactive and point people to good material. Let your youth know where they can go. There are actually many ministries which are dedicated to doing excellent and creative work for this generation. You can point people to these sites, friend them on Facebook, post links on your websites, add them to your email lists, and find creative ways to send them towards good information. Use the internet to be a positive influence.

**BE THE SOURCE.** It is our new reality that youth are growing up in a more anti-Christian society. They will face questions and criticisms of their faith and beliefs. It will come from friends, teachers, professors, and now the internet. Part of being proactive is becoming the source of information yourself. Instead of young people hearing about objections to our faith for the first time from anti-Christian sources, let them come from you.

If our young people need to be prepared to give an answer for what they believe, we need to help them do exactly that. Do not hide the objections people have. We need to tell them what they are. Our young people should not be surprised, overwhelmed, and destroyed by what they hear at university, high school, or the internet. Sheltering them from this until they are seventeen or eighteen *does not work*. Prepare them. Teach them to stand. Help them to discover answers for themselves.

**TAKE TIME FOR QUESTIONS.** No matter what kind of programs you run, at some point you need to provide an opportunity for students to ask questions. There must be time given for discussion. This is a needed part of every person's learning process. It is how we make what we are hearing part of our own beliefs. This is also an opportunity to hear what questions your youth are wrestling with. Hearing about their thoughts and struggles will give you a chance to go find some of those answers so you can better prepare them.

Here are a few suggestions for how you can hear the questions young people really have. Have question boxes. It can even be anonymous. You can do this online, or with an actual, physical box. You can set this up on your websites as a way for youth to ask questions they may not be comfortable saying in front of a group. It is also easy to set up anonymous online surveys where you can find out thoughts, beliefs, and questions people have. One such free online tool is www.surveymonkey.com.

In the end, though, our goal needs to be to create a place where people know they can ask questions. Do all you can to let people know they can ask without judgement or criticism. You can do this by continually letting them know that we are all in process in some way. Let them know that all people have questions and doubts. Even you. But together, we are working through them.

As parents, we need to make sure we give our children opportunities to talk to us about their questions and doubts. Do not simply leave it up to other people. Take on the responsibility to provide current, credible, and age-sensitive material for your kids. This can be through books, magazines, and even the internet. Again, hearing their questions gives you an opportunity to find answers and resources that can point them in the right direction.

## Opinion Is Truth

One of the biggest challenges with our new sources of information is that the content is fluid. More than ever, notions of truth, right, and wrong are all changing and in flux. Part of the reason this transformation is happening is that the internet presents opinion as truth.

Through the internet, a person with any agenda can promote their thoughts and beliefs. The internet truly is a source of free speech and ideas. This can be incredibly freeing as new thoughts, ideas, movements, and creativity will rise from this. At the same time, it can be incredibly damaging and dangerous as lies, hatred, intolerance, and wrong information is spread.

As a Christian, I am even embarrassed to discover what is on the internet in Jesus' name. The number of believers who have dedicated themselves to attacking other Christian ministries, denominations, and individuals is unbelievable. These open attacks are not only unbiblical, they are pour more fuel to the fire for those who already think Christians are hateful, intolerant, judgmental, and just plan ignorant.

When it comes to attacks against our faith from non-Christian resources, the things that are being said may or may not be true. They may be totally incorrect, they may be things that are taken out of context. At the same time, someone's objections may be true. Just as the Bible is our truth, this generation has its own version of truth. It is elastic and can be stretched in every direction.

As leaders and parents, we need to understand that this is the new reality. This reality requires a change in thinking, having only added to the already complex implications of having relative truth. The internet did not create this, but it is expanding it. On the internet, everyone's beliefs may be different, but they are all true—for them. This means we have youth who say they believe in the Bible, but it may just be true for them. They are totally comfortable with accepting more than one "truth" at the same time, even if they are different and even opposing.

## Advice

**TEACH WHAT TRUTH IS.** Let your children and youth know that opinion does not equate to truth. Talk about what the internet is. It is an open source for anyone to upload and disperse information and ideas, both right and wrong. In the end, all "truth" needs to be measured by the Word of God. In an age where this type of thinking is being challenged more and more, we must keep going back to the source and teach those we are leading to do the same. Tell your youth not to simply accept what someone says, or what they read. Instead encourage them to examine it next to the Bible.

## What Goes In Must Come Out

If it is true that what goes must come out, we should be concerned. From a young age, our children and youth have been ingesting a steady diet of whatever messages their media has been serving them. This comes through the movies and television they watch, the music they listen to, the information they read, and what they are taught. Their information also comes from friends who have grown up with the same messages. The mediums are numerous.

The amount of time young people spend "plugged in" is absolutely staggering. There are young people who are literally plugged in almost every minute of every day to some type of media source. It is not uncommon for youth to be listening to music, playing video games, or communicating online for six to ten hours a day.

Music, video games, television, movies, or social media are not in themselves good or evil. They are means of conveying a message. The questions we have to ask for our own children and youth is this: what messages are they hearing? Knowing what these messages are is vitally important, especially when the time they are listening to other voices greatly outnumbers the time you spend talking to them. This is true of parents, generational workers, and churches.

Parents and guardians need to become proactive. They need to be aware of the media their children are ingesting. They need to be aware of the time spent on this. Guidelines and controls can be established easier when our youth are younger. It is hard to go backwards, so start now.

## The Outflow

Besides the changing views of truth and faith, there are numerous other results of our constant exposure to secular media. There is a new and evolving view of sexuality. The present revolution may outdo the free love movement of the seventies. The things which were once hidden are now in the open.

Pictures, video, movies, and music are being freely passed around to and by children and youth. The ability to transfer information electronically has almost made any type of rating system ineffective. What was taboo or off-limits is now easily accessed, and is just seen as an alternative.

A constant and distorted view of sexuality is being presented to our children and youth. The ages when people are being exposed to graphic sexual messages has dramatically decreased. The vast majority of the messages this generation is hearing is that premarital sex, multiple partners, same-sex partners, voyeurism, and promiscuity is normal—and even expected.

If these are the messages our youth hear, whether it be for five hours a week or as much as fifty hours a week, how do we respond? Will the one-hour sex talk our kids hear once a year at youth group be able to counteract the thousands of hours of opposing messages? Not likely. An entire generation of young people is struggling with this issue, caused in part by increasingly sexualized media. More than ever before, we have teens and young adults addicted to pornography, masturbation, sexting, sexually-charged online chat, and promiscuity. Many feel there is no way out.

The results of being bound in this way, or becoming sexually involved with people in and out of the church, causes many to fall away. In an earlier chapter, we talked about how many people feel like they are a failure or a disappointment to God. This is one of the major snares that has been set for this generation. The guilt, addictions, and poor views of sexuality being picked up are affecting relationships, marriage, and a healthy sex life.

## Protecting Relationships

Constantly being plugged brings about changes in relationships. You can now have a car of parents and kids all traveling in a car together all listening to their own music, texting to their friends, existing in their own bubbles. They may be together by proximity, but not in reality.

As individuals and families, we need unplugged moments and time. We have to that our time for conversation and actual interaction. A healthy lifestyle includes time for God, family, friends, fun, exercise, and rest. We have to ensure that our urge to be plugged in does not rob us of these times. Technology is good when it is adding to our lives, not when it is robbing us of these needed things.

We cannot stop change. It is here, and there is much more coming. Communication forms have changed, and will change again. Instead of seeing everything as an enemy, we can redeem and embrace forms of communication. We can also make sure we are part of this revolution. Text your kids. Give them messages. Write them letters and emails. Use technology to communicate positive messages.

Our children and youth need to know they can talk to us about the struggles they are facing. In the end, this is likely the most important thing we can do. Brett Ullman, one of the world's top speakers on media and youth, wrote the following advice:

> The one thing I challenge parents more on these days is the idea of unconditional love. I spoke at a Christian school recently and after I got home I received an email from a student. She had heard me during the day and her mom had heard me at night. She wrote that her mom came home and talked about the stupid speaker who talked about the stupid issues that only idiots would deal with. The girl's letter went on to say, "I guess I am the idiot." She talked about all her struggles and how she does not feel like she can talk to her mom.

> Unconditional love means that we love our kids forever and always. Sometimes we are destroying this with our words. If my daughter Zoe ever gets pregnant in high school (she is only eight years old now), I want her to come and talk to me. I might not be happy about it, but I would rather her come to me than be alone on some doctor's table without me. I will love her no matter what. We need to look at how we can make sure our kids know we love them unconditionally.

> – Brett Ullman
> www.brettullman.com

## Advice

**POSITIVE MEDIA.** At a young age, try to introduce children to good media sources. Introduce them to contemporary music that matches their tastes. Take them to concerts of Christian artists. Go out of your way to make sure all or some of their choices are positive.

**WAITING.** A child does not need to be online and plugged in by any means possible. You do not need to shelter, but we are called to protect and help our kids make good choices. We need to be sure to let our kids develop ideas, thoughts, and grow without the constant perverse, violent, and explicit materials that now surrounds us. Put off introducing children to some media and communication forms. We also need to limit the time they spend surfing the web, texting, and playing video games.

**ONLINE GUIDELINES.** There are dangers involved with being plugged in. Sadly, there are people who use the internet to abuse, take advantage, and exploit children and youth. Teach your kids and youth to know how to protect themselves. Warn them of the dangers before they start. This should be something both parents and churches do.

## Resources

**INTERNET ACCOUNTABILITY.** There are now many great software applications which can filter and block inappropriate material from your computers. There are also programs which are available to provide accountability where a second party will receive your internet history. Either of these can be helpful. Some examples are Covenant Eyes (www.covenanteyes.com) and X3WATCH (www.x3watch.com).

These alone are not total solutions. Much of the information mentioned when it comes to faith does not fall under offensive material. Also, we are moving into a new era where the internet is available on most handheld devices, where a lot of software is presently dedicated to home computers. In the end, nothing replaces you personally checking on, being aware, and talking to your own children.

**MEDIA SPECIALISTS.** Have Christian media specialists come to talk to your church, parents, and youth. Another alternative is to take your youth and parents to events where these people are speaking. You can arrange these activities between a few churches. I would encourage you do to this annually to constantly equip parents and youth as media forms rapidly change. A good example of a safe and helpful site is www.brettullman.com. Do not just take your youth; involve parents and guardians as much as possible.

# The Bible and Other Religions

# 10

# The Bible and Other Religions

# 10

It seems like nothing ever stays the same. Even change changes. It changes speed. It changes intensity. Changing one thing can bring a multitude of changes to many other areas of our lives. Change is the acceptable norm. It makes our entire lives fluid. It can make us feel like we have nothing to hold onto. Sometimes it leaves us wishing that something would just stay the same.

When we look at the statistics of when most people seem to stop attending services, there are obvious trends. According to researchers and many studies, the largest drop-off occurs around the age of eighteen. However, that is not the only drop off point. What is clear from looking at the statistics is that the greatest times of loss occur at times when life is changing the most. Periods of great change coincide with big transitions in life.

---

> **"**
> I am a college student away from home and I've come to discover that there really is no place like home. I cannot seem to find a church that I am happy with. Besides that, it is a very long walk to a suitable church and work. I only go when I get to go home, which isn't often, and it is wonderful. I miss it so much.
> **"**

## The Loss of Constants

The constants in our lives are where we can find our foundation in this ever-changing existence. These constants are factors in keeping us focused and on track. They are our guides so we can know if we are going in the right direction. These constants don't come easily, and seem to be taken away so quickly.

When you join a new group of people, it takes time to feel like part of the group. It is through our activities and interaction with others that we develop our connections and friendships. In time, we gain feelings of acceptance and groups of people become a kind of family or tribe. This isn't instant. Sometimes it takes time to find these soul connections.

For those who have grown up in the church, or have attended for a period of time, these relationships have developed over time. Our Christian friends, church, and groups are part of our family. Many of our youth have support circles. They have their natural family. They have their youth group. They have leaders and staff members. They have a multilayered support system.

Whether someone has one or many support circles, at certain points all can be lost at once. This certainly accounts for why there is such a dramatic loss around graduation and the first year of college or work. Young people can face the loss of family support, the influence of their church family, and the disappearance of other circles of influence—all over night. Each of these have likely played a vital part in their ongoing spiritual well-being. These are not easily replaced, as some took a lifetime to develop.

Change and growing up are certainly inevitable. No matter how hard we try, we will always lose constants. There are many times in a young person's spiritual formation when they may face the loss of numerous constants. Some churches lose youth between Junior and Senior High. We know we lose a lot in the transition immediately after High School. We also lose many in the transition from college to work. Some studies have suggested that the percentage of drop-off here is as high as the percentage of high school graduates.

If we know these are points where we lose the most, we need to make these our focus. For example, when a Christian young person goes to college, the first weeks are of utmost importance. For most, if they do not connect with some kind of Christian community in the first few weeks, most likely they will not attend any church or group throughout their college years. I believe this is also true for people who move into a new area for work after high school or college. If there is not an intentional connection in the first few weeks, many will stop attending church. When we understand the importance of these transition times, we must deal with them accordingly.

The starting point must be recognizing the importance of these constants. Next, we need to identify what these are for the young people we are working with. For some people, they will be the programs. For some, it will be the leaders they have. For others, it will be family, either natural or spiritual. The next step is for us to prepare our youth to deal with them and to make sure they never have to face a loss of all of their constants at once. The good news is there are many very easy and practical things we can do to ease these transitions.

Nigel Cottle also talks about these transitions points. According to him, each transition point is

> ... a place where people have to make new time priorities. They will ask, "Why am I part of this church?" and "How important are the church activities in light of my recent life change?" Because transition points are destabilizing (and there are so many of them in the young adult years) it is critical that the church can answer the "Why am I part of this church?" question well.

As we try and answer this questions we will wrestle with the thoughts of this generation about the church, including, "What difference does this church make in the world around us?" and then "What part do I play in making that difference?" The church needs to have a compelling reason [for us] to belong to it.

## Advice

STAY CONNECTED. In this age, there is absolutely no reason we cannot stay connected. It would be absurd to imagine a son or daughter leaving for college, university, or work and a loving parent never communicating with them again. However, as church we do this to our spiritual family and children all the time. This in itself shows how shallow some of our relationships can be and the importance of us adopting people.

At minimum, every church family should continue to follow up, encourage, and keep in touch with its members until they are firmly established in a new location. This job could seem like a lot of work, but even a monthly email would keep communication open. It should be built in to any youth/young adults workers job description that there is at least minimal follow-up once youth leave for college or work.

BE PROACTIVE. Parents and leaders should do everything they can to connect their own children, and those they lead, to ministries where they are going. We often take care of helping to pick courses, getting books, and finding places to stay, all the while forgetting to plan for their spiritual life. Do research and find a few places for them to attend and connect.

If you are driving your own children to college, plan on attending a church with them their first Sunday. Help them to make those connections. Model the importance of finding a place for them. We know the importance of making these connections in the first few weeks, therefore this must be a priority.

**CALL AHEAD.** Every leader cannot follow their young people wherever they are going. However, there are many other great ways to help make connections. Contact the local groups, ministries, and churches in the area. Most universities have Christian groups or churches who are working on that campus. For the most part, they are led by people who have a huge heart to minister to students. They will follow up with people they are told are there. These can be found through your own denomination or by doing internet searches for groups operating at almost every university and college.

**DO YOUR PART.** You may not have students leaving, but you may be on the other side. Perhaps your church or ministry is located near or on a campus. Knowing the importance of connecting to students in the first few weeks of being in class, ask yourselves what you are doing to connect to these students. Local churches, campus ministries, and various groups need to be on campus in some way during this critical time. You can use flyers, posters, advertising, social media, random acts of kindness, events, and information booths to get the word out. The beginning is letting people know that there is a place to connect. Do your part.

**SELF-FEEDERS.** I do not believe we are meant to live out our Christian lives on our own. We need the support of others. At the same time, we can teach people to be completely dependent on others to feed them spiritually. This, in the end, is very detrimental. Along with accountability, we need to teach people to be responsible for themselves.

When my kids were young, they couldn't feed themselves at all. We had to prepare formula, food, bottles, and put their food in their mouths for them. As they got a bit older, they tried to feed themselves—and it was messy. It didn't always end up in their mouths, but on their faces, clothes, hair… and even on the floor. In time, they learned to pick up their own fork and spoon and feed themselves.

It would be just plain weird for me to now feed my twenty-one-year-old son the same way I did when he was one. If I did, I would actually be doing him harm, because it would mean I never taught him to take care of himself. However, when it comes to the spiritual lives of our youth, if we never teach them how to feed themselves, we cause them to remain as infants.

We cause maturity to develop when we teach people to take on spiritual habits. These habits can include things like Bible reading, prayer, time alone with God, rest, connecting with other Christians, and being in accountability circles. As our young people age, we need to wean them off milk and teach them to care for themselves. This can be done over many years, but all our programs need to be geared toward releasing spiritually mature people, not dependents.

**RECOGNIZE "WHO" THE CONSTANTS ARE.** Earlier in this book, we talked about the importance of parents, spiritual parents, and adoption. We have to recognize who the constants are for our youth. When we know who they are, we need to release these people to follow up, pray, encourage, and stay connected to our youth.

These constants should first include Christian parents, which we have already talked about. Then, for many, it will be a spiritual parent or influence. This could be a friend, leader, or pastor. These people need to be encouraged to stay connected in some of the ways already mentioned in this chapter. For example, if there is not a parent to call ahead to a university, a pastor or leader should do it.

These constants are also very important in local church settings as we face the results of times of transition. A Junior High leader should do all he or she can, not just welcoming the new people into their group, but also making sure those they were ministering to are connecting to the Senior High group. This again speaks to the importance of looking at all these age-segregated ministries as a whole, not individually, so we know if people are falling through the cracks.

**GOING TO COLLEGE SEMINARS.** We know our young people will face challenges to their faith when they arrive on campus. We know they will face new challenges to their values, beliefs, time, habits, and sexuality. So many young people are overwhelmed by their newfound freedom, opportunities for both good and bad, and experimentation.

There are many great courses and ministries that specifically deal with preparing our youth for these times. However, armed with a few good resources any leader, parent, or pastor can also take this on. If you have students leaving for work, college, or university, plan some time to discuss the challenges they will face and help prepare them.

### Life Will Change

Getting older has its challenges. As I mentioned, I have been a bit of an extreme sports fan and participant most of my life. Falling, wiping out, and getting hurt have always been a normal part of life. I am now noticing that I don't bounce back quite as quickly. Even my centre of gravity seems to be changing as more of my weight seems to be finding its way to my stomach. I know this is part of getting older, but I don't like it.

It is apparent that lots of people just do not want to grow up. Or at least they don't want to take on the responsibility and work that seems to come along with adulthood. Sooner or later, though, age catches up with most of us. It is not an easy transition.

If we want a certain career, we are going to have to work, study, and give up years of our lives dedicated to learning. We will likely go into debt doing it. When it is time to move out, we are going to have to get a job, if not before. We may even have to do this while going to college or university. Life always seems to get busy for most people. For young people, they are entering a season where they are facing new expectations, responsibilities, and time commitments they have never had before.

These challenges of time can follow people into marriage, new jobs, and the introduction of children into their lives. Many people do not know how to deal with the "seasons" they are going to go through. It may seem that they have never known a time in their lives without transition. Many Christian young adults get frustrated with themselves because it is impossible for them to do what they were doing before.

There are those who feel like they are failing God somehow, because of the season they are going through. They may have been very involved in their church, youth ministry, or campus ministry but have now hit a roadblock because they realize they cannot fit everything into their lives anymore. There may actually be some prioritizing that needs to happen, as even this is part of the learning process towards maturity. However, it may be that they simply can't do what they did before, and they may just need to hear that it is okay.

Life does bring changes, but they aren't all bad. Priorities change, and while this can be a negative, it can also be a positive. For example, when you have your own children you may not be able to be out doing ministry or hanging with friends five nights a week like you did when you were eighteen. However, God has given you some new young disciples to focus on. These are the seasons we go through, and it is alright to transition. It does not mean you are letting God down.

Our youth will certainly go through many seasons. Times of working too many hours. Times of extreme study. Times of extreme change. It is here where the voices of loving constants can bring a light of sanity and balance. Part of preparing people for this time of life needs to include preparing people for changes of season.

When I look or think about my children, I desire nothing but the best for them. Sometimes they come to mind and I just have to pray for them. I would give up anything for them. Looking back twenty years, though, I know I didn't think the same way. I have transitioned priorities, which I recognize now are good things. God gives us new priorities and responsibilities, and some old things need to be let go so that we can embrace the new.

I simply cannot be out doing all the things I did when I was single, even the things I did for God. It is not wrong if I can't. At this time, I am in a season of parenting. It is God-given and not something to fight. I am not a failure to God or anyone else, because I am here. However, I have heard and know of so many people who struggle with these feelings through university, when they enter in the workforce, in marriage, or when they have children. Let this be part of our preparation for our young people before they go to college. Prepare them to recognize what their priorities are through all life's seasons.

## New Freedoms, New Failures

With age comes responsibility, and also freedom. Part of our development and maturing comes from curiosity and experimentation. There is no shortage of ways this happens on campus. It is almost expected that young people are going to partake in all that is being offered. It is a time to expand their minds, to have new experiences, and to enjoy newfound freedoms. Drinking, parties, drugs, and sex will be available and offered.

To even think that these have no pull on youth who have grown up in the church is foolishness. These challenges are just as strong for them, if not worse than it is for their unchurched counterparts. Many have never had to stand on their own and have not developed the skills they need to make right decisions on their own. Some will stay strong in the face of temptation and many will fail. The results of partaking in these newfound freedoms often result in slavery and pain.

This is one reason we cannot just shelter our children. They will face temptation. Everyone does. We need to be able to teach them to make good and Godly decisions.

Each temptation has its challenges for our young people. However, nothing has the power to destroy spiritually like sexual issues. I have seen and heard countless examples of youth people and young adults whose lives were completely altered because of the relationships they became involved with. These spiritual and emotional connections can be carried for a lifetime.

This is a battlefield that causes many people to simply give up on faith. No matter what the cause—self-esteem issues, curiosity, a desire to fit in—many young people's spiritual lives seem to fall apart when sexual failure sets in. This is a day when sexuality is sold and promoted at a young age, and the temptations are everywhere. Our youth are told that it is normal to sleep around, to have multiple partners, to have same-sex relations, and to view pornography.

There is likely no issue that causes more guilt and condemnation amongst our young people. Whether it comes from thoughts, what they are viewing, or actual sexual activity, all these are having an effect on our youth. In an earlier chapter, we discussed how people who feel like failures will in fact give up because they are miserable. This is so true. Far too many young people are so caught up in addiction, bondage, and now guilt that they do not believe they can come back. In their minds, they have passed the point of no return. They have failed miserably and given up hope. For some, a life of promiscuity is more important than living for God.

This is not a subject that can be adequately dealt with in a small section of a chapter in one book. While this is not a new issue, we must at least recognize how constantly sexually stimulated this generation is through television, music, movies, the internet, and personal experience. Be aware of how much of an issue this is. Talk to your youth about relationships, sexuality, and their effects. This should be a regular part of any youth and young adult ministry.

## Advice

**PRAYING FOR GODLY SPOUSES.** I recently attended a wedding for a young couple I have known for a few years. They are both people who have a deep relationship with God. During the reception, several of the parents shared that through their lives they were praying for their own children but also that God would be preparing the person whom their child would be marrying. I believe we saw these prayers come true. This is a practice parents should adopt. Pray that God will prepare the people your children will marry. Pray that He would send someone that will love God, treat them right, and care for them in every way, even spiritually.

## Resources

**BEFORE YOU SAY GOODBYE.** This book contains much of the same material as the one you are reading now, but with ideas and advice for them to follow. There is also a study guide so that youth, college, or small groups can use it as a curriculum. For more information, visit www.davidsawler.com.

# This is Life

11

# This is Life

# 11

The thief comes only to steal and kill and destroy; I have come that they may have life, and have it to the full.

– John 10:10, NIV

Jesus came to give us life. Not just eternal life, but real life today. He came to restore us so we can now live out who we were created to be. We can live our lives for His purposes, doing the good works He has prepared for us to do. We can live in relationship with the God who spoke the very universe into existence.

Here, though, is where a huge number of our younger generation find themselves. (If we were honest, a huge number of Christians of all ages are in the same place.) They do not associate being a

Christian, or their church experience, with "life" at all. Rather, they are more likely to believe it is a lack of life.

They may believe the part about eternal life. However, even by that definition they may be thinking it just means they will exist in heaven, even unsure if that part sounds all that great. A huge number of people are not thinking of a life today filled with joy, happiness, purpose, or fulfillment.

When we go back and think of the story of the sower, we are fully aware that the enemy wants to see people fall away. This issue blinds people to the truth. It is a lie that being a Christian and living for Jesus means we are going to live a life void of happiness, fulfillment, and any enjoyment. In short, people believe that being a Christian is going to suck. People have believed that when Jesus said, "Take up your cross," it means all pleasure in life is over. That is not likely what Jesus was referring to, though.

### Bored?

One comment I have heard repeated from this generation is that they are simply bored in church. I am sure this is not a new issue, as other generations likely have struggled with this. However, just as Moses led the Israelites out of Egypt, we need leaders, ministers, and churches to lead this generation out of the land call Boredom.

Just as the Israelites needed deliverance from oppression and slavery, many in this generation have been bound and need freedom. Some people are trapped in beliefs that lead to wrong expectations of what this new life is about. There are churches and people who have become slaves of systems, traditions, and practices that don't work. Many are trapped as their leaders, and churches have never equipped or released them to do anything about it.

Here again, we are discovering that there is a disconnect between this generation's beliefs and church attendance. If you ask a church attending young person questions like, "Does Jesus' life seem boring?" the answer is most likely going to be, "No," or "Definitely not." You could even ask, "Do you think the disciples were bored?" Again, you would most likely hear, "No." However, if you ask, "Is church boring?" the most common answer will be, "Yes."

Is seems we may have succeeded in turning the most exciting news in all of history into something that is putting people to sleep. I hate to even admit this, but a big part of the problem may be us. I do not believe our faith is meant to be coma-inducing.

> "
> I quit attending church because I started to personally feel like churches are failing to do what the Bible holds them to do. By the Bible's standards, churches are supposed to be organizations to help the unfortunate.
> "

## Why Bother?

At certain points we seem to lose large percentages of our young people. The largest drop-off seems to be around the time people graduate. This is also a time when many people start working or going to college or university. While we may wonder why so many leave at once, it may be a false statistic in some ways. Many of these young people in fact disengaged many years earlier. They were just forced or compelled to attend services while their parents or guardians still had influence in their lives.

The issue of boredom is one that many seem to identify with. We have a generation which has been raised on change. They don't even know about life without the internet, social media, high-definition television, and endless entertainment. Everything around them changes constantly. This certainly is a challenge to churches, or any group that run events that are repetitive and highly predictable. Just as we would never go to the same movie two, three, or several hundred times, they do not want to go to the same church event over and over again.

It would be wrong, however, to simply assume that changing styles, music, or traditions are a sure-fire way to reach and keep a generation. Churches do need to make sure they are actually engaging people in their communities. If no one has been added to your church in years, or even months, you should be alarmed.

In fact, there are many examples of different types of churches doing incredibly well. Both traditional ones and those that are very contemporary. We also see lots of examples of both types failing. Even those who go off to plant and start new churches or faith communities do not all make it.

However, we also have a responsibility to make sure we are not only catering to one generation and forgetting the whole body. We have to make sure each generation is being spoken to by our methods. If our traditions and practices are hindering us from being effective, it may be time to let some of them go.

Many churches have attempted to fight boredom. Some have succeeded outright, some have succeeded for a time, and some not at all. In the end, unless you get to the root of why people are bored, your attempts will only be so effective. There is one thing that truly destroys boredom, and that's purpose.

### Advice

**MEANINGFUL MINISTRY.** While this has already been mentioned, it needs to be repeated. Do not give token ministry just to give someone something to do. Give away responsibility. They may fail, but they need an opportunity to learn, grow, and gain purpose in the church.

### Why Am I a Christian?

If you want to know if people understand their purpose, a good starting point is finding out if they know why they are Christians. For many, it is to receive eternal life, which is God's gift to us.

Many people say they are believers for the simple reason they have to be or else they will go to hell. Some are Christians because of the benefits that come with it. Some say they're Christians because they were born into it.

If someone doesn't know why they are a Christian, their faith will remain shallow and can easily be destroyed. Bringing this question up to any age group, especially this younger generation, is an opportunity to dispel wrong thinking and create roots that go deep into the soil. You may want to start by examining your own thoughts and ideas.

Many people are stuck in that land of boredom because they have never wrestled with this question. They aren't sure why they are in a church other than that it is necessary. It is there Christian duty or it is their family tradition to go every week. They may even know they have been saved from something, but that is as far as things have progressed.

Being saved from our sin, past, and separation from God is the beginning of our new walk with Christ. He picks us up, cleans us off, and saves us from a lost eternity. But many have never moved past what they were saved from. This was only part of Jesus' message: *"'The time promised by God has come at last!' he announced. 'The Kingdom of God is near! Repent of your sins and believe the Good News!'"* (Mark 1:15) We have heard about a prayer of repentance, but there is more.

We are, in fact, called by God to participate in His kingdom adventure. It is through repentance that we enter in. Repentance is the door in. However, there is so much to explore. We need to also believe the Good News that the Kingdom of God is near. Our lives as Christians are not simply about what we were saved from. Our lives are about what we have been saved for.

## This Is No Spectator Sport

When people associate boredom with their Christian walk, it is usually because their only context is church services. This in itself is a huge problem. I am a pastor and yet I find many of the services I go to dreadfully boring. If that is all I had, I wouldn't want to go, either. We must make sure our children's Christian experience is not totally wrapped up in sixty to ninety minutes on a Sunday morning.

Large group settings are inevitably at least partially spectator-based. Jesus taught and crowds listened, so this model is not wrong. It's improper, however, for this to be the only experience people have. We have clear Biblical teaching that there will be those who have the ability to teach and preach the Word of God. In the book of Acts, we see that this was part of what the early church did. *"All the believers devoted themselves to the apostles' teaching, and to fellowship, and to sharing in meals (including the Lord's Supper), and to prayer"* (Acts 2:42).

While this is a part of our walk of faith, it is just one of the parts. When people only experience this one facet, it leads to many feeling bored and unneeded. Unfortunately, churches have been guilty of either only presenting spectator-based events, or promoting them as the most important things they do. In Acts and the rest of scripture we discover that the early church devoted themselves to other things as well.

They devoted themselves to each other. They even shared their possessions. They met together in the temple and in their homes. They encouraged and prayed for one another. They encouraged each other to do good works. The confessed their sins to each other. They were involved. In Colossians, we read:

> Let the message of Christ dwell among you richly as you teach and admonish one another with all wisdom through psalms, hymns, and songs from the Spirit, singing to God with gratitude in your hearts. (Colossians 3:16, NIV)

It seems there was a part of even the early church model which was certainly not spectator-based. Everyone seemed to have a part. We also see this in what Jesus modeled. Jesus taught the crowds but lived in community with the disciples. It was in this setting where they asked questions, discussing the meaning behind what they had heard or saw.

Teaching with no application will always lead to boredom and feelings of purposelessness. This is not just a church issue; it is the same in most settings. As a church, we cannot just feed people and give them no way to express their faith outwardly. One of the reasons many of our own are struggling with church attendance is that they want to be the church, but they aren't sure how they can do that in church.

In essence, many people are desiring to be what we have taught them to be. However, they are refusing more teaching until they can at least apply something they have heard. Continued teaching without an outlet brings more frustration. This is why many in this generation are wrestling with questions like, "Does attending church services have anything to do with Christianity or my walk with God?" Or, after seeing no outcome after years of attendance, they may ask, "What does singing three songs and listening to a sermon every week have to do with living like Jesus?" It does not mean they haven't grown or absorbed knowledge; it means they have matured to a point where they want to reproduce and be fruitful. They will not be content to just attend. While they may have grown a little bit, we actually stunt or stop their growth if they never get a chance to express their faith in real and tangible ways.

Our purpose as believers must go beyond church service attendance. This alone is not a sign of growth and maturity. You will know if a tree is healthy if it produces good fruit, not just if it is found in a forest. This generation has no desire to be a statistics in a crowd. If they are going to be part of a church for the long-term, they must be interactive members.

## Advice

Involving people in ministry can only happen if we are intentional. In order to show people that our Christian walk is more than a Sunday experience, it needs to be modeled. As a church, in small groups, as classes, and as individuals we need to walk with the younger generation, showing them how to express their faith in different ways. As people grow, our ministry must move to help them discover their own gifts. We must then equip and release them to minister in those settings.

## Saved for a Purpose

Purpose does, indeed, fight boredom. When people are on a mission, they are willing to do things they wouldn't in normal circumstances. People on a mission sacrifice, give, invest, and pour themselves out. When we have a reason to do something, our perspectives on what we are doing change.

We have been saved for a purpose. As believers, we are a holy people. This means we are set apart for God. So many look at the scriptures that teach on this and think they refers only to what we don't do. While that may be a part of it, it misses the point. We are not to primarily be known for what we don't do. Too often, all people know is that we don't drink, smoke, or sleep around. Depending on what church background you are from, your list may be much longer.

Being set apart for God speaks more about what we are going to be used for than what we aren't. Now that our lives are dedicated to Him, we become active participants in Kingdom life. As believers, we are to be known for our love, our good deeds, and for turning communities around.

> " I can tell you why I'm looking at the exit sign in my church; I see very little Biblical precedent for the current church system—the whole 'Sunday morning, get a good seat, sing, give, listen, shake hands, go to lunch' mentality. "

We have been saved to help people be set free from addiction. We have been saved to tell of the incredible things God has done. We have been saved to bring good news and hope to the poor, and to the world. We have been saved to live a life of worship. We have been saved to live in the joy, freedom, love, peace, and fulfillment God brings. We have been saved to live out the mission of Jesus. "Life" is living for a purpose.

When we understand we have a purpose, we begin to take part in the things that move us along to seeing that purpose fulfilled. This will include corporate teaching, worship, ministry, and fellowship. Finding our purpose helps us to understand the meaning to some of our practices, helping us put aside things that aren't helping. When people regain the purposes for what they do, it reconnects their faith and their practices.

## Living the Church

When I think about how we have a generation that wants to be involved, interactive, and participate, I am given hope for the future. It is time to release the sleeping giant. There is no limit to what can happen when this generation is released to be the church in this world.

Our Christian walk is certainly meant to be an adventure. If our young people are not being challenged in our churches, we need to quickly readjust. The good news is that you do not have to come up with all the answers yourself. Ask your youth what they are feeling they should be doing. Then help them do it.

Let them see that their church is a place where they can be empowered, released, and equipped to do the things God is calling them to. Why many leave is that they feel it can't happen there. Let your church become a breeding ground for ideas, discussion, and ministry, *"and let us consider how we may spur one another on toward love and good deeds"* (Hebrews 10:24, NIV).

> **"**
> I want to do some real stuff. I want to go visit the homeless and the sick, and I want to learn how to love unconditionally. I want to actually live like Jesus, instead of doing a bad job of pretending.
> **"**

Our goal can never be to teach people to go to church. Our goal is to teach people to *be* the church. When we confuse the two, we present something that is empty. When we understand that our purpose is to be the church today, more will stay in their churches. As those leading, we have to make sure we really are promoting *being* more than *going*.

## It Is Life

Living for God is life. Our lives should be the overflow of love, Kingdom thinking, and Kingdom experience. We serve a living God, which means we have a living faith. It needs to move us, transform us, and take us places we would never imagine.

God has given us an invitation to be part of who He is and what He is doing. He is the most powerful and creative being in the universe. The outflow of being in a relationship with Him will cause things to happen. It is time that our own people believed that the gospel is in fact "Good News." In order for this to happen, they need to know and experience Him.

Encourage relationship with God. Speak on it. Teach it. Live it. It's not a relationship simply based on fear, tradition, religion, or their parents' faith; it's a relationship based on the saving knowledge of Jesus. Lift Jesus up, let them fall in love with Him. Young people need to have genuine God moments.

Model what Kingdom life looks like. As a group, whether as families, ministries, or churches, embark on Kingdom adventures together. There is incredible power in letting people get a vision for themselves of what purposeful Kingdom living looks like. When the people have purpose and vision, there is life. Without it, people perish.

## Advice

**SET UP GOD MOMENTS.** While we do not control the work of the Holy Spirit, we can certainly point people in the right direction. Set up activities and events where our children and youth will be likely to have encounters with God. Some of these can include individual and family prayer times—or concerts, retreats, camps, worship times, Bible reading and study, and so on. Be intentional in setting up a few activities a year which will be pivotal experiences for your children and youth.

# Conclusion

12

# Conclusion

# 12

As Solomon examined his own life and the world around him, he came to several conclusions. One which he repeated, over and over, was just how meaningless he felt everything was. He felt that if we spend all our days working for something, and yet have no one to pass it on to, it is not only meaningless, but also depressing.

Some people have made the mistake of looking at the statistics of our retention of youth and become overwhelmed and depressed. Or perhaps it is even closer to home, because you are dealing with your own children and those you minister to. You may even have some who are not serving God today. Or perhaps you are wondering where those who are will be in a few years.

I want to encourage you. You can be a great influence in what happens next. Despite what has been, despite the former shortcomings on a personal or church level, the future is still wide open. In fact, I fully believe that we have been looking at some of these numbers and statistics completely wrong.

God is very much in control. The church is not dying. Many denominations will, in fact, lose many of their buildings, and some may even cease to exist. Perhaps God is even removing some things from us so that we can get our eyes back where they should be looking.

> **"**
> I want truth, freedom, and above all love. Real love. His love. The synopsis of the message of Jesus was simple—love God, love others. I think if we stop wasting our time and resources on building these ridiculous empires and programs, and simply live *real* day-to-day Jesusanity, the world will gently shake at its foundations.
> **"**

When I think about what we have to pass on to people, there are things far more valuable than passing on our buildings and programs. There are things we can pass on that are eternal. Things that matter far more. Your faith, your time, your care, your grace, your wisdom, and your love. These mean far more than any material thing.

Invest into the things that last. Invest into what means the most. As a parent, pastor, and church, our most valuable assets are our children and youth. My prayer for the church today is that the hearts of our fathers and mothers will truly turn to the children.

For our young people, our desire must be that this *"generation should set its hope anew on God, not forgetting his glorious miracles and obeying his commands"* (Psalm 78:7). They need to have a real relationship with God, a relationship that is theirs. We can point, pray, and direct, but in the end it must become their faith.

Even when I think of the frustrations many youth and young adults have with the church today, it may be an opportunity. This is a beginning where many will recreate new forms or expressions of the church. These will be places and groups that will effectively reach into the world and bring the gospel to the new generations. Those who remain in our churches will be able to teach and challenge us to be people who value them and release them into ministry.

Over the next few days and weeks, look back over the words, stories, and ideas in this book. I would encourage you to just start with one idea, given by many of the contributors, and put it into practice. In time, keep trying more. Some will work for you and some won't, but try something.

On a personal level, each of us needs to decide to be a person of positive example and influence. We can decide to be the spiritual fathers and mothers we need to be for our own children and those around us. We can be people who bless this generation and speak life over them. Pray for our children and youth. Pray that God will equip you to help those around you be fruit that remains.

# Contributors

**ASHLEY BEAUDIN** is a freelance writer and activist. She is a visionary with a desire to walk out Kingdom passion in the areas of intimacy with Jesus, intergenerational unity, and international justice. She believes God has something to say and He won't be silent about it. (www.ashleybeaudin.com)

**NIGEL COTTLE** is the Young Adults Researcher for BYM (Baptist Youth Ministries) in Auckland, New Zealand. He is deeply concerned about the missing generation—young adults—in their churches. He, with his family, is involved with planting a missional church in the inner city suburb of Kingsland. There's never a dull moment in Nigel's life!

**MARCEL DEREGT** is the leadership development director of Youth Unlimited. Youth Unlimited helps churches challenge youth to commit their lives to Jesus Christ and transform their world for Him. (www.youthunlimited.org)

**MARK GRIFFIN** is presently serving as a global worker in Southern Germany, planting a network of churches with a generation of emerging national leaders. He is also a speaker, coach, ghost writer, and editor. (www.markgriffin.ca)

**JAKE KIRCHER** has been working in youth ministry for nine years and is currently the youth pastor at Grace Community Church in New Canaan, Connecticut. He is also works with REACH Youth, New England, doing regional training and web design. He is a graduate of Gordon College and has a B.A. in Youth Ministry and minor in Biblical and Theological Studies. He is a local coordinator for the National Network of Youth Ministry and has been published in Youth Worker Journal, NNYM.com, and Relevant-Magazine.com.

**JONATHAN LAMBE** is a youth pastor, speaker, and writer from Bermuda. He is also the CEO of Kingdom Reign Ministries, which empowers teens and young adults to holistically identify their purpose and develop a strategy to live a successful life. (www. reignlive.com)

**DON MANN** is a pastor, teacher, and equipper. He is the founder of the ministry Reinventing the Church, whose vision is to equip church leaders worldwide to transition to the next level of effectiveness for the twenty-first century. (www.reinventingthechurch.com)

**SEAN MCDOWELL** is the head of the Bible Department at Capistrano Valley Christian Schools, where he teaches courses on Philosophy, Theology, and Apologetics. His apologetics training was awarded Exemplary Status by the Association of Christian Schools International. Sean is listed among the top 100 apologists. He is also a popular speaker at camps, churches, schools, universities, and conferences nationwide. His books include *The Unshakable Truth* (co-written with Josh McDowell) for parents and youth workers, and *Is God Just a Human Invention?* (co-written with Jonathan Morrow) for students and adults. (www.seanmcdowell.org)

**PASTOR MIKE MILLER** pastors Shiloh Youth. At age nineteen, he had a vision to serve at his home church and returned to be taught and discipled under the leadership at Rock Church. In 2004, Mike was placed as Outreach Pastor and founded Go Missions International. In September 2006, he was placed as Youth Pastor where he serves today. (www.shilohyouth.ca)

**JIM MOLLOY**. This chapter was coauthored by Jim Molloy, who wrote a paper entitled "Farewell Youth Pastor?" He is a life coach and currently serves as the Executive Director of Ministries and Missions for the Pentecostal Assemblies of Canada, Maritime District. He is also the author of *Every Leader's Everest*, a book about insecurity. (www.leaderscripts.wordpress.com)

**CAREY NIEUWHOF** is the lead pastor of Connexus Community Church, a multi-campus church north of Toronto and strategic partner of North Point Community Church. Before starting Connexus in 2007, Carey served for twelve years within a mainline denomination, transitioning three small rural congregations into a new congregation that experienced significant growth. He speaks to church leaders across North America about change, leadership, parenting, and the strategy behind Orange, a ministry dedicated to helping parents and churches raise Godly children. Carey co-authored *Parenting Beyond Your Capacity* with Reggie Joiner. He and his wife Toni live near Barrie, Ontario and have two teenage sons, Jordan and Sam. In his spare time, you can find him cycling his heart out on a back road somewhere. (www.careynieuwhof.com, www.orangeparents.org)

**JEREMY POSTAL** has spent the last ten years serving in youth and young adult ministry at Christian Life Community church in Abbotsford, British Columbia. He can be reached at jeremy.postal@gmail.com. (www.twitter.com/JeremyPostal, www.clcc.ca)

**ADRIAN THOMAS** leads Every Day Ministries in the Dominican Republic. He presently works with hundreds of pastors, bringing to them resources and training. After spending many years as a youth pastor, he now bring teams from all over North America to minister in that country. (www.everydayministries.com)

**BRETT ULLMAN** is introduced as a top expert, speaker, and author on media influences. He travels North America speaking to adolescents, leaders, and their parents on topics including sexuality, substance abuse, and self-injury. Driven by a desire to discuss, explore, and share the Christian reality of living in a media-saturated world, Brett's seminars engage and challenge attendees through high-impact, technology-driven presentations. (www.brettullman.com, www.worldsapart.org, www.yourstory.info)

**DAVID WELLS** was elected as general superintendent of The Pentecostal Assemblies of Canada (PAOC) in May 2008 after serving as the district superintendent of the BC/Yukon district. He serves as chair of the board for the Evangelical Fellowship of Canada and has been a constant voice to challenge churches to reach this generation. (www.paoc.org)

# Resources

Barna, George. *Revolutionary Parenting: Raising Your Kids to Become Spiritual Champions* (Carol Stream, IL: Tyndale House Publishers, 2010).

Baxter, Jeff. *Together: Adults and Teenagers Transforming the Church* (Grand Rapids, MI: Zondervan, 2010).

Cunningham, Sarah. *Dear Church* (Grand Rapids, MI: Zondervan, 2006).

Dale, Felicity. *An Army of Ordinary People: Stories of Real-Life Men and Women Simply Being the Church* (Carol Stream, IL: Barna Books, 2010).

Devries, Mark. *Family-Based Youth Ministry* (Downer's Grove, IL: InterVarsity Press, 2004).

Devries, Mark. *Sustainable Youth Ministry: Why Most Youth Ministry Doesn't Last and What Church Can Do About It* (Downer's Grove, IL: InterVarsity Press, 2008).

DiMarco, Michael & Hayley DiMarco. *Almost Sex: 9 Signs You Are About to Go Too Far (or Already Have)* (Grand Rapids, MI: Revel, 2009).

Dobson, James C. *When God Doesn't Make Sense* (Carol Stream, IL: Tyndale House Publishers, 1993).

Groeschel, Craig. *It: How Churches and Leaders Can Get It and Keep It* (Grand Rapids, MI: Zondervan, 2008).

Groeschel, Craig. *The Christian Atheist* (Grand Rapids, MI: Zondervan, 2010).

Hammett, Edward H. *Reaching People Under Forty While Keeping People Over Sixty* (Danvers, MA: Chalice Press, 2007).

Holmen, Mark. *Faith Begins at Home: The Family Makeover with Christ at the Center* (Ventura, CA: Regal Books, 2005).

Hanby, Mark. *You Have Not Many Fathers: Recovering the Generational Blessing* (Shippensburg, PA: Destiny Image Publishers, 1996).

Johnson, Rick. *Better Dads, Better Sons: How Fathers Can Guide Boys to Become Men of Character* (Grand Rapids, MI: Revel, 2006).

Joiner, Reggie. *Think Orange* (Paris, ON: David C. Cook Distribution Canada, 2009).

Joiner, Reggie & Carey Nieuwhof. *Parenting Beyond Your Capacity* (Paris, ON: David C. Cook Distribution Canada, 2010).

Kinnaman, David & Gabe Lyons. *UnChristian* (Grand Rapids, MI: Baker Books, 2007).

Mansfield, Stephen. *Rechurch: Healing Your Way Back to the People of God* (Carol Stream, IL: Barna Books, 2010).

Mayo, Jeanne. *When He Feels Far Away* (Oviedo, FL: Higher Life Press, 2009).

McManus, Erwin Raphael. *Soul Cravings* (Nashville, TN: Thomas Nelson, 2006).

Mueller, Walt. *Engaging the Soul of Youth Culture: Bridging Teen Worldviews And Christian Truth* (Downer's Grove, IL: InterVarsity Press, 2006).

Rainer, Thom S. & Eric Geiger. *Simple Church: Returning to God's Process for Making Disciples* (Nashville, TN: B&H Publishing Group, 2006).

Rainer, Thom S. & Eric Geiger III. *Essential Church* (Nashville, TN: B&H Publishing Group, 2008).

Sawler, David. *The Disciple* (Winnipeg, MB: Word Alive Press, 2010). Visit www.davidsawler.com. This is an extensive study into what Jesus modeled and taught those following Him.

Schadt, Jeff. *Going, Going, Gone: Protecting Teen's Hearts that Are on the Edge* (Colorado Springs, CO: NavPress, 2010).

Sowers, John. *Fatherless Generation: Redeeming the Story* (Grand Rapids, MI: Zondervan, 2010).

Yancey, Philip. *Disappointment with God* (Grand Rapids, MI: Zondervan, 1988).

Yancey, Philip. *Church: Why Bother?* (Grand Rapids, MI: Zondervan, 1998).

Youth Transition Network (www.Ytn.org). This organization has many resources available for parents, leaders, and pastors to help students navigate through their college years.

www.weloveouryouthworker.co.uk

## Apologetic Websites

www.bethinking.org

www.thetruthproject.org

www.apologetics315.blogspot.com (has a large list of material and authors)

www.ezrainstitute.ca

## Apologetic Authors and Books

Each of these authors has many books. I have only mentioned a few.

Arterburn, Stephen & Roger Marsh. *Internet Protect Your Kids:- Keep Your Children Safe from the Dark Side of Technology* (Nashville, TN: Thomas Nelson, 2007).

Boot, Joe. *Why I Still Believe* (Ada, MI: Baker Book, 2006).

Burns, Jim. *Teen.ology: The Art of Raising Great Teenagers* (Minneapolis, MN: Bethany House Publishers, 2010).

HomeWord Center for Youth and Family—www.homeword.com

Keller, Timothy. *The Reason for God* (New York, NY: Penguin Group, 2008).

Lewis, C.S. *Mere Christianity* (New York, NY: Harper Collins, 1952).

Little, Paul E. *Know Why You Believe* (Downer's Grove, IL: InterVarsity Press, 2008).

McDowell, Josh. *The New Evidence that Demands a Verdict* (Nashville, TN: Thomas Nelson, 1999).

McDowell, Sean. *Apologetics for a New Generation* (Eugene, OR: Harvest House Publishers, 2009).

Strobel, Lee. *The Case for Christ* (Grand Rapids, MI: Zondervan, 1998).

Strobel, Lee. *The Case for Faith* (Grand Rapids, MI: Zondervan, 2000).

Zacharias, Ravi & Lee Strobel. *The End of Reason: A Response to the New Atheists* (Grand Rapids, MI: Zondervan, 2008).

Zacharias, Ravi. *Who Made God?* (Grand Rapids, MI: Zondervan, 2003).

For more information, resources, and videos please go to:

www.beforetheysaygoodbye.com

www.davidsawler.com